KU-048-485

Hildasay
to Home

Hildasay to Home

How I found a family by walking the UK's coastline

CHRISTIAN LEWIS

MACMILLAN

First published 2024 by Macmillan
an imprint of Pan Macmillan
The Smithson, 6 Briset Street, London EC1M 5NR
EU representative: Macmillan Publishers Ireland Ltd, 1st Floor,
The Liffey Trust Centre, 117–126 Sheriff Street Upper,
Dublin 1, D01 YC43
Associated companies throughout the world
www.panmacmillan.com

ISBN 978-1-0350-3378-2

Copyright © Christian Lewis 2024

The right of Christian Lewis to be identified as the
author of this work has been asserted by him in accordance
with the Copyright, Designs and Patents Act 1988.

Plate section photographs: pp. 1–7 courtesy of author;
p. 8 © Adrian White/SSAFA

All rights reserved. No part of this publication may be reproduced,
stored in a retrieval system, or transmitted, in any form, or by any means
(electronic, mechanical, photocopying, recording or otherwise)
without the prior written permission of the publisher.

Pan Macmillan does not have any control over, or any responsibility for,
any author or third-party websites referred to in or on this book.

1 3 5 7 9 8 6 4 2

A CIP catalogue record for this book is available from the British Library.

Map artwork on p. *ix* by ML Design Ltd
Typeset in Fairfield LT Std by Palimpsest Book Production Ltd, Falkirk, Stirlingshire
Printed and bound by CPI Group (UK) Ltd, Croydon, CR0 4YY

This book is sold subject to the condition that it shall not, by way of
trade or otherwise, be lent, hired out, or otherwise circulated without
the publisher's prior consent in any form of binding or cover other than
that in which it is published and without a similar condition including
this condition being imposed on the subsequent purchaser.

Visit **www.panmacmillan.com** to read more about all our books
and to buy them. You will also find features, author interviews and
news of any author events, and you can sign up for e-newsletters
so that you're always first to hear about our new releases.

To my dearest Jet

My favourite parts of this whole adventure were always with you. For years I thought your legacy would be that you were the first dog to have achieved what you have and to have raised over half a million pounds for charity. But I was wrong. Your real legacy is the fact that you dictated the pace of the walk and, in doing so, led me to Kate and then to Magnus. Whenever I look at them, it will always be you to whom I am grateful for this wonderful family. You will forever be missed and there won't be a single day that I won't look back with the fondest memories. I love you.

Contents

Contents

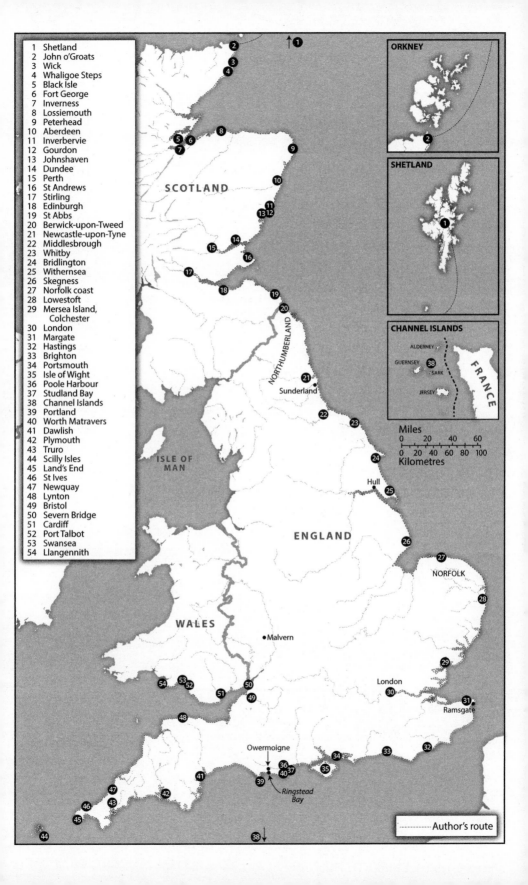

1 Shetland
2 John o'Groats
3 Wick
4 Whaligoe Steps
5 Black Isle
6 Fort George
7 Inverness
8 Lossiemouth
9 Peterhead
10 Aberdeen
11 Inverbervie
12 Gourdon
13 Johnshaven
14 Dundee
15 Perth
16 St Andrews
17 Stirling
18 Edinburgh
19 St Abbs
20 Berwick-upon-Tweed
21 Newcastle-upon-Tyne
22 Middlesbrough
23 Whitby
24 Bridlington
25 Withernsea
26 Skegness
27 Norfolk coast
28 Lowestoft
29 Mersea Island,
   Colchester
30 London
31 Margate
32 Hastings
33 Brighton
34 Portsmouth
35 Isle of Wight
36 Poole Harbour
37 Studland Bay
38 Channel Islands
39 Portland
40 Worth Matravers
41 Dawlish
42 Plymouth
43 Truro
44 Scilly Isles
45 Land's End
46 St Ives
47 Newquay
48 Lynton
49 Bristol
50 Severn Bridge
51 Cardiff
52 Port Talbot
53 Swansea
54 Llangennith

ORKNEY

SHETLAND

CHANNEL ISLANDS

ALDERNEY

GUERNSEY

SARK

JERSEY

FRANCE

SCOTLAND

NORTHUMBERLAND

Sunderland

ISLE OF
MAN

ENGLAND

Hull

NORFOLK

WALES

Malvern

London

Ramsgate

Miles
0   20   40   60
0 20 40 60 80 100
Kilometres

Owermoigne

Ringstead
Bay

- - - - - - - Author's route

PART ONE

Life Changes

1

The sweetshop is
open again!

A quest for happiness in my life and to raise money for
SSAFA, the armed forces charity, began on 1 August 2017
on Llangennith beach on the Gower Peninsula. My aim
was to walk the entire British coastline, and that meant
the mainland, every inhabited isle, plus as many uninhabited islets that I could get to. At the beginning, and
for much of the walk, I had less than ten quid in my
pocket. I had to rapidly learn the art of coastal foraging
in unforgiving Scottish weather, as well as come to the
realization that I would need help from perfect strangers
en route if I was to complete this mammoth quest, not
least with their fabulous generosity in replacing my tent
each time the Scottish wind ripped another one and sent
it to the tent cemetery.

I was in the Shetland Isles when the first lockdown

was ordered in March 2020. Beside me was my dog and best friend, Jet, whom I had been lucky enough to adopt earlier on in my walk. Together we spent three and a half months on Hildasay, an uninhabited island an hour and a half out to sea. There was no electricity, no fresh water, and no gas there. A fisherman would drop off water and food supplies by boat, but otherwise I had to forage. It was here I realized I had finally found respect for myself, as well as discovering resilience and discipline on a level I hadn't experienced since being in the Parachute Regiment. More importantly, however, after walking 12,000 miles, I had found the grail I'd been searching for, and something I had long lacked: happiness.

It was now the beginning of June 2020, and lockdown was finally over. Victor, who had been monumental in helping bring over fresh water and supplies while I was on the island of Hildasay, pulled up to the tiny harbour in his private four-man boat ready to take Jet and me back to mainland Shetland again. The swell of the sea made me anxious; even though I was in good hands, if anything were to happen, I knew that helping Jet was beyond my control. The North Sea, despite it being June, was still freezing and wouldn't heat up until gone September. Jet and I had crossed rough seas many times to get to different islands, but despite all the experience, it never seemed to get any easier.

'Chris,' Victor said, 'it's going to be bumpy! We had better leave immediately as the winds are picking and we won't be able to cross.' I threw our gear on board (with a real sense of urgency I may add), picked up Jet and carefully stepped down onto the boat so as not to trip and faceplant onto the deck. As soon as feet and paws were safely on board, Victor fired up the engines and pulled away from the concrete harbour. Within five minutes we hit open sea and the side-on waves rocked us around for the hellish forty-minute journey back to land.

I sat at the rear of the boat with Jet clamped between my shins in a bid to stop her sliding from side to side uncontrollably. We each hated it as much as the other, but I knew Jet found real comfort in being with me just as I felt comfort being a passenger with a Shetland fisherman who knew his stuff. About fifteen minutes into the journey, I turned my head to look back at Hildasay. In a voice that was almost a whisper, both sad and fearful (given the swell), I said, 'Goodbye, mate. Until next time.' I felt a lump in my throat and a tingling sensation ran through my body as I uttered the words; I was sad to be leaving.

Saying goodbye was bittersweet – like bidding farewell to an old friend who I'd gotten to know incredibly well and wouldn't see again for a while. I knew every nook and cranny of that island. It would always be the place where I had picked up the shattered pieces of my life and put them all back together again – and this time welded with steel, not fragile glue. I'd gotten stronger and fitter out there, learned all I could about foraging, hit my fundraising target of £100,000 for SSAFA, and got to watch Jet be a completely free and happy dog. The chimes of thousands of birds both in the morning and at night had become so embedded in my mind that any time I wanted to hear them, all I had to do was close my eyes and imagine! The island was such a special place. I would be a liar if I didn't admit to being proud for taking on the challenge of living out at sea alone on an uninhabited island for the whole of the first lockdown. And not only had I survived; I had thrived.

'Bye, pal,' I said one last time before turning my attention towards the front of the boat. I took a deep breath, looked down at Jet and gave her a big wink. 'Jet, it's time. Let's go and nail this fucking thing once and for all!'

I estimated we still had around three weeks left to complete Shetland, which included three more islands (two inhabited and one uninhabited), plus a small chunk of mainland Shetland. We had survived the winter relatively unscathed and spring had now well and truly sprung into action; flowers, plants and wildlife were appearing in abundance, and the winds, though still strong and relentless, no longer felt like I was being stabbed by tiny pins all over my hands and face – it was now more like a gentle slap from a warm hand! In all, things were looking up!

By the time we arrived back at the harbour of Burra (another island off Shetland now joined to the mainland by a bridge), I had flicked a switch in my head back to 'walk mode'. I spent a day or two sleeping in Victor's son's garage, which had a small room out the back with a shower and sink where I cleaned, gutted and cleared out all of my equipment, ready to continue. To me, doing this was like having your house completely gutted, with a car valet to boot! I'd become incredibly anal about my equipment; everything had to be in its place, cleaned and ready to use any time at a moment's notice. It's vital if you want to be a good adventurer! It always felt amazing when it was all done, as well – such a satisfying feeling; I loved it.

The three months we'd spent cast away on Hildasay had done Jet and me a world of good: a forced but needed rest from the relentless years of routine – packing away the tent, putting the tent back up – the hard graft of walking from one place to another every day and the constant focus and problem-solving to get us through whatever stood between A and B. I now felt more ready than I'd ever been for the challenge ahead. So far, I had walked from Swansea, completed the west coast of England, the formidable west coast of Scotland, both the inner and outer Hebridean islands, the north of Scotland, Orkney and its surrounding islands, and most of Shetland.

I had a goal, a purpose, and I felt good mentally and physically. At this point, only an asteroid wiping out humanity could have stopped me from finishing this walk.

Before continuing, I spent an evening with Victor and his wonderful family to say goodbye. We dined on the herring that had come into season and been caught by Victor's boat, washed down with beer and whisky as we celebrated what I believe was a beautiful connection between the Lawrences, Jet and myself. Together, we had all achieved something great – I could not have done it without them. Ted, Jamie and a few others who had also helped me came over to enjoy our last gathering before I set off the next day. That evening, as we all gathered round the fire, I toasted the endless efforts they had made, bringing food supplies and fresh water whenever the weather permitted. It was the most beautiful night with the most amazing people who had played such a special part in this adventure. Above all, I had once again made new friends.

After those months sleeping on a mattress in a house on Hildasay – albeit one with no running water, electricity or heating – it was amazing to be back in a tent again after lockdown and once again be surrounded by the comforting orange canvas that had kept us protected from the elements for the past three winters. On my first morning back on the walk, I stared down the coastline that I was about to undertake with newfound enthusiasm and a fresh glint in my eye. I took a deep breath, released it slowly while looking up to the sky, then turned my attention down to Jet: 'Come on, mate, let's bloody nail this.'

I found a pallet washed up on the beach and, after smashing it up with a boulder, used the wood to make a fire. I was immediately back in the swing of things. I sat next to the fire, Jet huddled up in the tent cocooned in my sleeping bag, and got the maps out, ready to get moving the next day. It felt good to be back – all the coastline I had been staring at for months from the island of Hildasay was now mine to conquer. I was like a child who had been looking through the window of the sweetshop for three months, only to find it closed every day. Now, it was like the door had finally opened – I was allowed in and so excited to explore!

Fresh and ready to go, and with a new fundraising target of £200,000 – which I had decided upon on Hildasay, after hitting my original target of £100,000 – this unpredictable, unplanned expedition was back on and firing on all cylinders. After finishing Shetland, I would return to the northeast tip of Scotland ready to head south. All I had left to walk was the east coast of Scotland, the east coast of England, the south coast of England and its islands (the Isle of Wight, the Channel Islands and the Scilly Isles), what remained for me of the west coast of England and then finally back into Wales, to finish at Llangennith beach on the Gower Peninsula, where I had set off on 1 August 2017.

In my mind, nothing else on this walk could trump the hardships of surviving the Outer Hebrides in a tent in winter followed by Shetland in a tent the following winter. Nothing the south had to offer could be in any way as challenging, I thought. But, oh – how wrong I was! Like any adventurer, you just never know what's around the corner. Little did I know that, very soon, by a simple twist of fate and the universe's impeccable timing, my life was about to change for ever.

2

King Magnus and the ancestors of Foula

My next stop was the island of Foula, about an hour and twenty minutes' boat ride from the west coast of Shetland. Foula is around 2.5 miles long by 3.5 miles wide and home to around thirty-five inhabitants, some of whom are indigenous to this small piece of land. It also lays claim to having the second highest sea cliffs in the UK, beaten only by Conachair on St Kilda. The cliffs tower some 1,220 feet above sea level, giving rise to a monumental cliff face. One man even base-jumped off the top of them a few years before my arrival! It has one small school and a special breed of sheep with brown-tinted wool, free to roam wherever they please. I was really excited to explore the place.

Being on an island, locals were incredibly worried about any outsiders coming over so soon after Covid. People on the mainland had warned me that I may not get the best reception when I arrived, or even be allowed off the boat for that matter! I really empathized with them if I'm honest – 'keep them all away' is exactly how I'd feel if I lived there. I tried my luck and headed for the boat to find around four locals who had made a trip over for supplies; the skipper, a lady and two other men stood around preparing to make the return journey. I took a deep breath and nervously headed towards them to ask for a passage over. I didn't get an immediate response and was asked to go and wait in the waiting room until they reached a verdict; after a few minutes I was reluctantly granted permission, but in no way did this subdue my worry about how I would be received on the island itself. Still, the hard part was done, and in no time, we set sail once again.

It was particularly windy – our biggest swell yet – and the waves lashed the side of the boat relentlessly. The already awful crossing was made worse by the fact that we had nowhere to sit. Jet and I were wedged in between a pallet of supplies and the side of the boat with just enough room to use my legs as a way of stopping us sliding around everywhere. The whole journey was dire: Jet was being sick and shaking with nerves and I couldn't get the thought out of my head that if one strap from the pallet broke, we would be crushed to death against the side of the gunwales. The skipper and his three other passengers chatted away casually. I wittered away too, like I didn't have a care in the world, but my arse was clenched as tight as Fort Knox.

It was around 2 p.m. that we pulled into the small harbour, and the sense of relief was monumental. Pre-lockdown, people would have been waiting at the harbour to greet us, but now things were completely different. Already feeling slightly unwanted, I had been told that one fella might be particularly 'funny' with me, a bloke named Magnus. I wasn't excited to meet him truth be told.

A man of average height, around forty years of age, with the appearance of a typical islander, hardy and weathered, watched on as we prepared to dock.

'Is that Magnus standing over there on the dock?' I asked one of the crew as he tethered the mooring ropes to the giant cleats on land.

'Yep! Lived here all his life,' he said.

Nervously, I disembarked, knowing I was the first tourist to step foot on this island in four months. A few people waited on the dock to unload the supplies from the boat that had been brought over from mainland Shetland. I was half expecting to get pushed back on! I said a quick 'hello' to Magnus, and attempted to read his response, but he gave nothing away. I then scurried away to find a place to camp, feeling rather seasick for the first time in my life. The crew and locals, including Magnus, said hardly anything at all. They were busy unloading the boat as I walked away. I felt so uncomfortable, I really did. *Let's get this island done and fuck off on the boat back to the mainland* was my only thought. I eventually spewed, got the tent up and readied myself for the next day.

A few hours later, now nestling into my sleeping bag, I heard a cough and the sound of someone wading through the long grass where I'd pitched my tent, only a few hundred feet from the harbour. I looked out to see Magnus heading towards me. I quickly pulled in my head and slumped back on the roll mat thinking, *Fuck – here we go!* I'd not been met with any hostility since leaving England, and the prospect felt soul-destroying.

'Chris!' Magnus shouted as he neared the tent. I got out of my sleeping bag and crawled out. To my surprise, however, he came forward and shook my hand. 'My brother owns a place on the north side of the island. You are welcome to stay in it if you like? My mother lived there but passed away a few years ago and it's sitting empty.'

I beamed at him, with relief as much as gratitude. 'Thanks, mate, I'd love that!'

'Great! My name's Magnus. Pack up your gear and I'll give you a lift to the house.'

As we chatted on the way down, I told him about my journey while he told me about his family and the island. After dropping me off and showing me round the old house, Magnus left me to it. I really didn't stay in houses on this walk; it was very unlike me, but I liked the idea of having somewhere to return after walking without having to get all my gear out for a change. Plus, I'd be alone, which was fine with me – I'm most comfortable in my own skin with my own shadow for company.

I'd been in the house for a few hours journaling when I heard a bang at the door. Magnus had returned, this time with a bottle of whisky – pretty standard for a Scot

I'd come to learn! I smiled, he smiled and before we knew it, merrily drunk, burping and darting, we were getting on like a house on fire, like we had known each other for years! We talked about his family and my walk, among other things, and he was great. Before he left, he pulled a photo album from the table in the living room. 'Chris, feel free to have a look through. There's some really old photos in there – it's genuinely interesting,' he said in his thick Shetland accent.

'Thanks, mate, I most certainly shall.'

The house, which was relatively small but perfect for a couple, was situated on the north side of Foula, which saw very little sun. All of the other islanders resided on the south side, meaning while I was here, I appeared to have the north of the island all to myself. The house was surrounded by fields that had once been croft farmed, and to the west, sea cliffs towered so high above that they blocked any sun during the winter months! It must have been a truly brutal place to live and work back in the day. I had so much admiration for such a harsh yet simple life that his ancestors must have lived.

I lit some candles as the sun went down, sipped the last of the whisky we had shared and got stuck in to the photo album. I'd been given some beautiful Shetland orchestral music to listen to, so I decided to put it on while I indulged in someone else's family history! It was a really special few hours, and I took stock and time to appreciate my position and where I was. As I flicked through, I got lost in the magic of the photos, some so old that cameras must have not long been invented. The black-and-white images of older Foula men and women sat around a cooking pot hanging from the wooden beams of the roof particularly caught my imagination. The weathered and solemn expressions on the gnarled faces of Magnus's ancestors really told a story of what life had been like back then. I bet most never even left the island.

To live a life on a tiny island like Foula, seeing the same few faces every day, is almost unimaginable to folks nowadays. The winds and harsh winters, as well as the solitude, mean it takes a special kind of person to be able to make a life here. I was transfixed by Magnus's photographs and had so many questions I knew I'd never get the answers to. Up until ninety years ago, the local church services were still conducted in Norn, a relic of the Old Norse language spoken by Vikings 1,000 years ago! I found it mind-blowing that there was still somewhere in the UK where a language as ancient as this had not only survived, but was in everyday use until as recent an event as the *Titanic* sinking in 1912! The whole place had a very peaceful and historic feel to it.

As I continued to flick through those moving snapshots in time, I noticed on looking at the captions that every generation of father bore the same name: Magnus. I loved it – hundreds of years of tradition passed on from father to son. The name itself has Latin origins and became very popular throughout Scandinavia. It was first introduced by the Norwegian king Magnus Olufsen back in 1035, and the name was carried over the North Sea from Norwegian Trondheim to our shores by the Vikings, and stayed put for over 1,000 years. I loved it and wished it was my name!

The island of Foula itself was beautiful. I was determined to climb to the highest spot of the sea cliffs to get a proper view, but on my first two attempts the mighty winds battered me down. My final attempt was a steep climb under constant and rather unnerving attacks from swooping bonxies (Arctic skuas). God, they were relentless! On the way back down from the top, Jet and I had to navigate through a minefield of these chicken-sized dive-bombing birds. Jet actually got so pissed off at the endless tirade that she snapped and went into hunt mode, jumping and aggressively attempting to take them down as they swooped for her. I'd never seen her like that before and admired her determination to fight back. I should have taken a leaf out of her book; the thought of feasting on one would have given me immense satisfaction after such an ordeal!

After three nights and with Foula now in the bag, having spent the entire time walking, looking at maps and prepping for the next island, it was time for us to move on. However, there were no boats going for a while! I put a post up on my 'Chris Walks the UK' Facebook page saying we were stuck and would have to wait another four days until we could return back to mainland Shetland. Jamie, the owner of the shop in Burra, who had been amazing to me while I was on Hildasay, got in touch to say he would be happy to come and fetch me and take me back over. This was a huge effort involving hours at sea just to get to Foula, not to mention the extra hour over to where I could get on the boat, followed by yet further hours back to the mainland. I wasn't sure I could let him go to such lengths just for us, but he was adamant and took to the water within hours. God, I was so grateful.

Jamie arrived on his twin-engine boat ready to take us back over in no time. The seas were much calmer this time around and would make for a much better crossing, to my relief! Magnus, his wife and children all came down to see me off. I was indebted to him for being so nice and felt I'd made another friend who would welcome me back any time. And, once again, I was reminded how important it is to keep your own opinion and not believe everything you hear. As we said our goodbyes, Jamie jumped out of his boat and alerted us that a fishing boat had run into trouble. The engines had blown and the boat was stranded a few hours out to sea – an awful position to be in. Without hesitation, he, his two crew and Magnus all jumped on board. What was originally a pick-up and drop-off had now become a sea rescue mission!

Jet and I stayed ashore so as not to get in the way and the lads sped off at full pelt to go and help. I was positive they would bring the stranded fishermen back safely. About four hours later, I could see the green starboard lights of two boats, and one in tow! The relief was epic. 'Well done, lads!' I shouted at the top of my voice. They arrived to a round of applause on shore as they made their way safely into the harbour. The winds can change up here in seconds; what was a horrible situation could have easily turned into a catastrophic one in no time. That boat coming to pick me up was obviously meant to be. Thank goodness! We went back to the mainland feeling incredibly lucky.

Papa Stour, a majestic island with a population of fewer than fifteen people living on 820 hectares of land, was the perfect end to the inhabited islands of Scotland, thanks to it being soaked in Neolithic, Viking and contemporary history – something I had become fascinated with during my time on the walk. It also had huge sinkholes in the ground, leading to sea caves the size of a five-a-side footy pitch, and looking down into the abyss gave me a real sense that humans should not enter such a dangerous place.

From there I began my final section of Shetland, back to where I started in Brea six months earlier. It was the last of my Scottish island adventures, and so a day of very mixed emotions. From here on, it was south towards England. The Hebrides, Orkney and Shetland had been without a doubt the most brutal yet fulfilling part of my journey so far – even my whole life – with beautifully friendly people who give you their time without restraint.

I have absolutely no problem in saying that there are parts of the UK that could learn a thing or two from the islanders! The pace of life is slower, and money is not their sole priority; rather, there's a simpler way of getting by – enjoying local music and each other's company, as well as everyone helping each other out. It was a way of living that really struck a chord with me. None of this not even knowing your neighbour's name nonsense! Instead, there was a real sense of community and pride in their land and origins, coupled with the most breathtaking landscapes and coastline the UK has to offer, mostly wild and unharmed by humans, where clean pristine waters are unpolluted by litter, burst sewage pipes or waste pumped out by water companies. In all, I saw these remote isles as much cleaner, healthier, happier places, where humans co-exist in a more mature and selfless manner. To me, it felt like stepping back in time – and for the better.

I arrived at the ferry ready to head back to mainland Scotland in complete surprise as to how many locals had come down to say farewell to both me and Jet. It was such a wonderful moment, though sad at the same time. I hugged each and every one of them to say goodbye as we walked towards the ship's door. Just like on the Hebrides and Orkney, I had arrived here a complete stranger to them, and them to me, but somehow, along the way, I'd made a massive connection with so many of them and left feeling like I was saying goodbye to friends and family. I had earned their respect and they had earned mine. We had a mutual admiration for each other and love for the land they lived on.

Jet and I stood outside on deck at the back of the Norse Link Ferry and as the ship pulled off from Lerwick, I waved to all the people who had come to see us off. The smaller they became the further we sailed away, I realized it wasn't just Shetland I was saying goodbye to, but the end of an era; a part of my life and my island adventures on this walk that had given me the freedom to just be me without all the white noise and constant distractions of my former existence. It was the first time in my life I had felt completely free – and what a feeling that is! The islands of Scotland had stolen my heart, and although this was goodbye, I felt some peace knowing that, someday, I would be back.

3

Chance encounter at the Whaligoe Steps

With the Scottish islands now completed, and with that a massive sense of personal achievement coursing through my veins, we landed safely back on mainland Scotland in July 2020. I loved the boat journey over. The connections I'd made had become more and more evident as the hours went by; as the boat sailed past the beautiful small island of Fair Isle, locals were sending me photos of our boat passing them with heart-warming messages of well wishes, and I sent photos of Fair Isle back to them. Never in my wildest dreams did I imagine the impact this journey would have on others as well as myself. It was such a wholesome feeling to say the least. It's funny, but I can safely say I have felt more a part of a community being a traveller than I ever had with anywhere I'd lived before.

Now, back in Thurso on the northern coast of mainland Scotland, it was a three-day hike along the coast to reach John o'Groats after completing the most northerly point of mainland Britain – Dunnet Head. I must admit, it didn't feel too special as I'd already hit the most northerly point of the whole of Britain back in Unst, Shetland, but either way, it was nice to get a picture by the sign. The most northerly, westerly, southerly and easterly points had always been my main targets to reach, but having ticked two of them off already on the islands, this simply didn't give me the same sense of achievement. I was excited, however, as the next day a friend, Dan Davies, was coming up to join me for a few days. This would be the first familiar face I had seen in years, not since the very start of my journey. Dan and I had met way back on the west coast of Scotland. He was doing the Land's End to John o'Groats route, but with some adventurous detours along the way!

From that first meeting, we would remain friends, good friends. Dan is a 6 foot 3 man with dreadlocks, with a kind of scruffy look about him and always in shorts – completely comfortable in his own skin! He's the kind of bloke that would drop anything in a second if anyone needed help. He really has a heart of pure gold. Aside from that, what I really loved about him was how creative and driven he is – always with a camera, a drone, a head full of knowledge and constantly smiling; it's safe to say he's probably the easiest person I've ever been around. And that takes some doing given the fact that I'd been isolated in a tent on my own with a dog for three years by this point! After hearing Dan had sustained an injury and was feeling understandably low about it, I invited him to come and see me for a few days. If anything, to give him some encouragement and a hoped-for morale boost.

We had the most amazing ten days, heading along the northeast coast of Scotland and down towards Wick. On the way, Dan insisted we celebrate my arrival back to mainland Scotland with some whisky each night by a fire. I loved every minute of it, and by taking this stretch slowly and just enjoying the long nights, without realizing it at the time, he had done me possibly the biggest favour a man could ask for. Had he not been there, I'd have easily been much further down the coast by this point. And had *that* happened, fate would never have intervened and blessed me as it would in only a week's time.

The day before Dan left to return all the way back to Bournemouth, he'd gotten in touch with some friends he'd met while on his own personal journey, Lee and Liza, who lived just out on the outskirts of Wick, northeast Scotland. Lee was away with work at this point, but Liza offered to come by and bring us some supplies with their young son, Archie. The night before I'd left to return to the mainland, Shetland's winds decided to give me one last tickle and a big storm snapped my tent poles, leaving me with a half-working tent; a total pain in the arse to try to pitch each evening, always using a tie I'd been given over there to wrap around the snapped tent pole to enable me to still sleep in it. Another storm and it wouldn't survive the night.

When Liza arrived armed with some food and, of course, in the normal Scottish style, a bottle of Jura whisky, Dan and I played with her son Archie for a while as we chatted to Liza. I took to her straight away. As had been the case so many times up north, she simply couldn't stop offering help with anything I needed and invited us to come back to hers for a hot meal, a shower and to sleep in a tepee that was already erected in the back garden. Given my tent situation and the fact I hadn't felt warm water on my skin since leaving Shetland, I lapped up the offer.

Dan left the next morning. Unbeknown to me, the night before while in the kitchen, Liza and Dan had been talking about my broken tent. After hearing about my situation, Liza had called her husband, Lee, and they both agreed to buy me a new MSR tent, exactly the same as the one I already had. Liza came out with some break-fast the following morning to tell me the epic news that, in just four days, my new tent would arrive at their house. Once again, I was completely blown away and lost for words at how wonderful people – and complete strangers at that – can be. I gave her a massive hug and we both agreed that I'd sit the next four days out, to eat well, do admin and sleep in the tepee until it arrived. I was so grateful and wished Lee was there so I could shake his hand.

Liza and Lee lived slightly off the coast, and after the third day, I felt a serious urge to camp up somewhere on the coast rather than be in a back garden. Don't get me wrong, I loved being there and playing games with little Archie, and I also felt that, since Lee was away, Liza

26

probably enjoyed having another adult around to talk to (which I completely understood). But the lovely relation-ship between myself and the coastline where I'd spent so much time was pulling me back harder with each passing day. So I asked Liza if she wouldn't mind dropping me off for one evening while we waited for the tent, on a part of the coast she liked and knew I could get some space to spend the night alone.

By this stage, national press had helped raise my profile to the point where anywhere I went – towns, villages or even just out on the coastal clifftops – I was being recog-nized and stopped with a litany of questions about my journey, with accompanying selfies to boot! I didn't mind at all, but, as I wasn't in this for fame or attention, there were times when it took its toll on me – more so at night, when folks occasionally shook the tent for a selfie at 10 p.m., when I was asleep! So long as I was getting some kind of time alone, I could manage the other.

With that in mind, Liza drove me down to a place around fifteen minutes from her house called the Whaligoe Steps, a popular tourist attraction with 365 handmade steps that lead down a 250-foot cliff to a beautiful little harbour at the bottom. Back in the day during the herring boom in the 1800s, men went out to sea to collect the fish and bring them back to the tiny harbour. Each day the women (fisherwomen as they were called) would then scale the 365 steps and walk 8 miles to the nearest town, Wick, to sell them. I loved the idea of camping down at the bottom. It would be my first night alone since Dan arrived a few weeks ago, or so I thought! Little did I know, this last-minute decision to camp down at the bottom of the Whaligoe Steps would change my life for ever. If only we knew it, our destiny is writ large in the stars above us.

Late that afternoon, Liza dropped me off in a small car park near the steps and headed off. As I walked towards the top of them, a fella called as he came outside of his house. 'So you're the famous walker, then! I'm Davy. I look after the steps. Anything you want to know, just ask me!' he said in the fastest, thickest north Scottish accent I'd ever heard. After a galloping fifteen-minute chat, I told Davy he was welcome to pop down after I'd pitched up and got sorted for the night. With that, I made my way down the steps with Jet and started the process of erecting my broken tent. Davy popped in for an hour to chat and tell me some of the history of the area. At this point, there was only about two hours left of light and still a few tourists about, but I knew they would all disperse soon enough and I'd have the place to myself.

A young lady in her mid-twenties who had recognized me from a recent news piece we had done for STV (Scottish Television) came over, and we chatted for about ten minutes about my walk, but mostly about Jet. Out of the corner of my eye, I noticed another lady, I'd say around thirty years old, looking over in our direction. I'd gotten good at clocking a potential question-asker by now! After walking over with a beaming smile, she brazenly interrupted our conversation: 'I'm so sorry to interrupt but I can't stay long here and I read on your tent that you're walking the UK coastline. How long have you been going?'

I looked up at the lady who was already chatting to me, almost apologetically for the interruption, before introducing myself and Jet to the intruder. She had dark hair pulled back in a bun, a purple raincoat and black leggings with pink socks pulled up over the top of walking boots. I noticed she had beautiful skin, and clearly took care of herself.

Our conversation lasted no more than a few minutes before she said, 'I have to go now as it's going to be dark soon and I need to find somewhere to pitch my tent before I end up fumbling around unable to see anything!' And with that, she just left. As she walked away, I glanced in her direction thinking, *What the hell just happened?!* One minute she was here and the next she had gone.

After saying goodbye to the lady I had originally been talking to, that was that. Finally, I was alone and ready to eat my dinner and listen to the sea to put me to sleep once again. Perfect.

About forty minutes later, however, I heard the pitter patter of feet slowly heading down the Whaligoe Steps. *More tourists?* I thought. There wasn't a lot of daylight left. *They won't be long,* I said to myself, *and then I'll be back on my own again.* I looked towards the steps from behind my tent, out of curiosity more than anything, and would you believe it – it was that girl in pink heading down the steps loaded with her backpack, tent and a bulging carrier bag!

'Chris!' she said as she walked closer to Jet and me, again with a beautiful beaming smile and as confident as on our last brief encounter. 'It's getting dark soon and I have nowhere to camp. Would it be okay with you if I camped down here by you for the night? You obviously know what you're doing!' she said with a chuckle.

'I thought you might be hungry, so I got us both some fish and chips with a couple of cans of Tennent's to wash it down. And a sausage for Jet obviously! Oh, and my name's Kate by the way.'

My very first thought was, *Shit, I've just eaten! I'm not going to seem ungrateful, though, so I'll have to eat them or devise a way to slip them to Jet!*

'No problem at all, Kate. You're more than welcome. Can I give you a hand pitching the tent? It's pretty windy and it'll be dark soon.'

'Nah! Don't worry, I got it!' she replied.

While Kate got to work pitching her tent (rather badly, I might add!), she told me about her mini adventure doing her 'off the beaten track' version of Scotland's North Coast 500 (500 miles of coastline that loops around Scotland), and wild camping, all alone, as a post-lockdown/birthday treat to herself.

'Wild camping in the north of Scotland on your own!? That's quite ballsy,' I said. 'You must love camping.'

'No, not really,' she replied. 'I'm a freezer and get so cold at night, plus I find it excruciatingly uncomfortable,' she laughed. 'But I love adventure so it's worth it!'

I smiled and totally understood where she was coming from. We sat down together to eat and cracked open a Tennent's. I'd positioned myself in a way where I could fake eat the odd chip and smuggle the fish to Jet, who was nestled behind me in the tent.

As dark closed in, the conversation between Kate and me flowed as easy as an estuary into the sea. The more we talked about adventure, the more it was evident that Kate and I shared the same enthusiasm for getting away and exploring the world. Each time Kate would tell me about some off-the-scale adventure she had always wanted to do, I was in disbelief at how similar my own ambitions were, whether it be trekking across Antarctica in the style of Shackleton, sailing around French Polynesia, hiking across continents, kayaking down uncharted rivers, spending weeks marooned on remote islands or off-roading through Africa. You name it, they were all on my list!

It was obvious she wasn't just a talker either, but a doer! Kate was very well travelled; she'd lived in Mexico and been around most of South and Central America, as well as visited Nepal, India and Vietnam, to name just a few. And many of these countries she'd gone to and explored on her own. In fact, that night she told me that in a few weeks, she was off to Afghanistan to go and scope out some possibilities for training teachers to improve educational access out there, having spent the past ten years as a teacher in early years education. She was also going there to climb some of the mountains in a remote region.

Afghanistan! I thought. *This girl really has some balls!* I was impressed.

As it got later, I could tell Kate was cold (I noticed how abysmal her kit was), and as any gentleman would, I gave her my Rab jacket, gloves and any warm kit I had. I was probably in my prime at this point when it came to being able to withstand cold, given where I'd just spent my last few winters. Never before in three years of camping had I invited anyone to my tent; my bubble, my home. But I felt incredibly comfortable around Kate, and even after only four hours of us meeting, I knew she wouldn't take my invite as anything sleezy or some kind of ulterior motive (and believe me, it wasn't). I was enjoying a conversation that didn't entail talking about my walk all the time, and Kate had no idea who I was or what I was doing when she approached me, which was refreshing and kept the conversation on more of a level playing field. It felt rare to sit with someone who got as excited as I did about forthcoming adventures, knowing full well, given her travelling background, that this wasn't just idle dreaming – she would actually do it.

We chatted and laughed into the early hours, sharing mutual stories of adventures, our favourite explorers and their exploits, Greek mythology, survival and the stars! I showed her Orion's Belt, the Milky Way, the Plough, Pegasus and some handy star navigational tips, then went into some of my foraging skills and tips for turning seawater into drinking water. She had some incredible stories herself and such a thirst for knowledge when it came to survival skills and adventure, we could have gone on all night.

As Kate was clearly still cold, I told her to grab her sleeping bag and bring it to my tent so she could tuck up inside it while I sat outside and we could continue talking. When she brought it over, I looked at her in disbelief.

'What the fuck is that?!'

'I know,' she laughed. 'My gear is atrocious. I've had this same sleeping bag since I was thirteen – it was twenty-five quid from Blacks in the nineties! It's useless!'

Essentially, it was a big hanky, and no good for man or beast.

'Oh dear. No wonder you get cold at night! Tonight you can use my sleeping bag when you return to your tent – you'll sleep much better! It probably stinks, but anything is better than that thing!'

She accepted without much hesitation: 'Thanks so much – that's amazing of you!'

Deep down, I was gutted. Jet and I would have to sleep with her spider's web of a sleeping bag now, but hey, I'd had the most wonderful night – it was the least I could do in exchange for her company.

We sat up talking until 3 a.m., when we eventually said goodnight and Kate returned to her tent with all my warm gear, including my sleeping bag! I wrapped Jet up in Kate's and went to sleep. The next morning, Kate was up early taking photos of the beautiful spot where we'd spent the night. I made us both a coffee. I only had one cup, so I drank mine from my cooking pot. We packed up and made our way back up to the top of the steps. I have to say I was pretty impressed with her stamina, going up all those steps carrying a heavy load.

'Kate, I'm not sure of your plans, but you're more than welcome to camp with us again tonight if you want. I'll get a fire on.'

'Oh, I'd love to,' she replied, looking at me directly, 'but

I can't. Today I have to drive back down south as I have work commitments I need to get back for. I have a packed schedule coming up, delivering start-of-term INSET days, and I've got to get prepping! Otherwise, I would for sure.'

'No problem,' I assured her. 'Just thought I'd offer on the off-chance!'

'I don't know if you'd like to, as I'm sure you get lots of requests for this on your trek, but if you're up for it, we could exchange numbers and stay in touch?'

I wasn't one to hand out my number easily, but on this occasion, it felt like a no-brainer. We gave each other a big hug and said our goodbyes. As she disappeared into the distance, climbed into her car and drove away, I was genuinely gutted to see her go. Which surprised me, given how much I valued my own space. I think it's safe to say that neither of us had any idea at the time, but this random encounter at the bottom of the cliffs would be the start of something truly life-changing.

4

Lady and the Tramp

The next section of the walk along the east coast of Scotland, heading for Edinburgh, would slowly but surely become a whole different ball game. Along the coastline, around 100 miles south from my location (sticking as rigidly to the coast as I was), would be Inverness, my first city since Glasgow. In fact, Inverness would mark my first city in nearly three years of walking! (Two years and eight months to be exact.)

Cities have their advantages – plenty of shops, plenty of people to promote the charity to and raise some money. But what I was looking forward to most about the east coast was the thought of a coastal path! My word – the difference it would make to both Jet and me! I'd barely have to check the maps! So long as the sun came up slightly behind me and in my face for most of the day,

I was heading south! All I had to do was follow a path! Just the prospect of having steps on the way down and back up the cliffs was a HUGE relief compared to battling my way through completely overgrown, tedious terrain, which was so slow and energy-sapping. That thought had been in my head as I pushed myself so hard around the many lochs, peat bogs, hills and mountains, and I was immensely excited now that day had come.

Another great advantage of passing villages, towns and cities that were much closer together than I'd been used to, was that with locals out walking the coastal paths and more and more amenities closer to hand the further south and back into civilization I got, if I were to get injured – be it a slip, fall or something more serious – then I'd never be too far from help and rescue, which was certainly a comforting feeling. This may sound over the top, but I'd concentrated so intensely and for so long on not putting a foot wrong, knowing that, in a lot of places I was walking, it would be incredibly hard to find me – and with little, if any, cell phone signal at times, I would have been well and truly screwed! It's an unnerving feeling (definitely not one of the perks of adventuring alone), but it also makes you feel so alive. It was a massive weight off my mind and a huge comfort to know that a lot of the physical dangers were now behind me.

As much as I could go on about the many different highlights of the stretches of coast to come, heading further south would also have some major drawbacks – the biggest of all being that once I crossed the border back into England, wild camping would become illegal.

Just as I had back in England over three years ago, it would mean a lot of sneaking about and no doubt I would be confronted with animosity once again. I dreaded the thought, and was doubly determined to make the most of the east coast of Scotland and enjoy every second of the freedom before it was stripped away from me for the remainder of my walk.

Fortunately, behind the scenes of my social media, something else was happening that provided a happy distraction from thinking about wild camping and the freedom to do so. The distraction's name was Kate Barron.

The day after Kate and I first met, I sent her a message to see if she had arrived home okay. In return, I received a photo of her having just woken up in the back of her car with her crazy bird-nest hair so stuck together now that it literally stood on end of its own accord – the best bed-hair I'd ever seen! I laughed out loud. The first night we met, I really admired that she just couldn't care less about how Worzel Gummidge she looked after nine days' wild camping! I loved that she just didn't give a shit.

As the days drew into weeks, the back and forth between us was pretty constant. We really loved listening to each other's stories of adventure and dreams of future expeditions. The more we kept in touch, the more I began to like her. Aside from the fact that she's incredibly beautiful, it was her fun-loving, energetic aura that really started to grab my attention. However, my one main thought was: *What on earth would such a beautiful, well-educated, well-spoken woman, who has an outstanding career as a teacher, who flies around the world travelling independently and training teachers in different countries, want with a man who's homeless, without any money what- soever and possesses nothing more than a tent and one set of clothes, and for the majority of the time stinks to high heaven of sweat, mud and all of the other day-to-day odours!?*

She was single, but she had been living the London life and travelled at any given opportunity; she was always meeting new people who I had absolutely no doubt would try to snap up such a wonderful catch. I felt a complete underdog in my head. I simply wouldn't have the slightest of chances. Perhaps they were my own insecurities or, having not known Kate long at all, a rather shallow perspective on who she was as a person.

I did my very best to try to supress my attraction to her and accept I'd just made a friend. But I couldn't, and my feelings would only get stronger.

One night, after a very long day of walking, I arrived in the village of Brora just before the estuary that would take me round to Bonar Bridge and then back up into Tain. I got cosied up for the night in my tent, settled Jet into my sleeping bag, and, like I did every night at this point, had a long phone conversation with Kate. I don't think she quite realized at the time just how much of a pain in the arse it was to charge up my phone for these calls. Now in more populated areas (at least in my eyes), I would have to organize leaving my battery packs with people everywhere and anywhere, so I could try to keep my phone charged. It was hard work to maintain our contact, but somehow, even with all the other logistical demands of the walk, I managed it.

After our conversation, Kate sent me a video on WhatsApp. 'Chris, I know you must be knackered after such a long day and I know how you love a story, so I'd thought I'd read you a bedtime story to help you get to sleep a bit easier! You never know – two verses in and you might be out like a light!' she winked. 'So I thought I'd read you the poem of "The Highwayman" to help you nod off.' I propped up my dry kit bag that had forever been my faithful pillow at night (incredibly uncomfortable, but I was so used to it by now) so I could pay full attention before turning in for the night.

Having just finished her working day, Kate was lying on her bed reading 'The Highwayman' to me some 400 miles away. The light showed all of her face and I noticed she had makeup on (I'd never seen her with makeup before!), and as she started to read the poem, I became lost in her, barely even hearing the words she was speaking. I just stared, with a voice in my head playing like a repeated record: 'You are the most beautiful woman I have ever seen in my life and here you are, late at night, after a long day working, taking your time to read me poems to fall asleep to.'

After watching it back-to-back about five times, I lay my head back on my roll mat, looked down at Jet and said, 'Pal, what am I going to do?' Jet just looked back up at me with those 'just go to bed, Dad' eyes, as she often did.

'I think I've fallen in love with her! Shit! She's in a different class to me! This is going to hurt if the feeling isn't mutual!' I chuckled, and with that, I switched off my head torch and went to sleep.

5

Stalker

I'd not been wrong about the east coast of Scotland being a world away from the west and the islands. All the way down to Inverness, the coastline had its cliffs, but it was far less wild and rather more well-kept if anything; agricultural land meant cows and sheep maintained the grassy hills to near perfection, making for short, easy-walking grass that followed the coastline, with small, quaint fishing villages spread out along the way. The A9 road that's used as part of the now very popular 'North Coast 500' driving route was never more than a mile or so away, and it would have been so easy to just plod down it and make great time, clocking up good mileage daily, but, true to myself and my word, I continued along the coastline going nowhere near it.

Jet was happy as Larry. I knew her inside out by now

and I could see she loved the short grass and less challenging terrain to scramble around on and sniff out fox
and rabbit holes. Now, deep into September, the summer
heat had calmed down and what I've always called 'storm
season' had begun to bring in colder winds and longer
nights. It was so much easier to sleep and gain some extra
miles each day now that summer was over, and I no longer
ran the risk of Jet overheating (I would never walk her
during the hottest hours of the day). She was happy as
could be, as was I. I almost couldn't believe that Jet and
I would never again have to cope with the endless barrage
from May to September of the relentless Scottish midges.
The east coast, because of the drier, less boggy and better-
kept land, proved far less enticing to the midge population
– a huge gift for us after what we'd endured over two
summers on the west coast! It was so lovely to be able
to sit outside at night with the tent flaps open and not
be a meal for them. Many times, hidden in a zipped-up
tent while boiling half to death, I'd dreamed of this
moment, and here it was! But Jet and I had beaten them,
the little bastards!

In her six-week absence before I saw her again, there
wasn't a minute of the day that Kate didn't make an
appearance in my thoughts. I'd become that pathetic
loved-up man who every ten minutes switched his phone
off airplane mode to see if I had a message. I'm not
ashamed to say it either. Most men (and women) who
have fallen in love have been through it whether they
admit it or not. And fortunately, almost every time I looked,
she had messaged! During this time I had never let on

how I felt; I didn't want to risk ruining such a lovely connection. As an outsider, if someone had told me that a girl they liked was constantly messaging and speaking for hours on the phone daily, I'd laugh and tell them, 'Of course she likes you, you fool!' But, as ever my own worst critic, I just couldn't see it. However, I was about to get my first sign that she might've just had a thing for this walking hairball in a kilt.

I made my way from Tain through Alness, down to Dingwall and around, towards Black Isle – my last section before hitting Inverness. I'd had so many people get in touch asking me to come over to see them, have dinner or spend the night, either camped up in the garden or in the garage (I made a rule never to sleep in houses). It was such lovely kindness; however, I was a fella who had fallen head over heels for the first time in my life. Sickeningly smitten with Kate, the last thing I wanted at the time was to spend my nights being hosted and asked questions about the walk. As generous as the offers were, my mind was elsewhere all of the time, and so, for this section, I just kept myself to myself and, very unusually for me, barely even posted on my page, so nobody knew where I was!

The day I arrived in Alness, it rained so hard the entire day that a lady called Sam, in her mid-fifties, who lived in a beautiful house just outside the town, offered me a shed and a place to dry all my gear out. More so for Jet's sake, I agreed on the condition that nobody would find out I was there. She explained she had a friend coming to stay who was an avid follower of mine, loved camping and would love to meet both me and Jet. I said that was fine – just nobody else if that was okay. Sam picked me up from the coast and drove us to her home. When we arrived, Jet and I headed straight to the shed down in the bottom of the garden to change into my dry kit and set up a bed space. To my disbelief, there was another roll mat, sleeping bag and a little gas stove already set out inside.

No bloody way am I sharing this! I thought to myself. To make matters worse, the 'friend' just happened to be more than an avid follower – if I'm honest, she was a bit of a stalker! I'd received constant messages over a long period of time from her: 'Can I come meet you? Can I come camping with you?', with the occasional hint of bunny-boiler, 'I want a man' talk! All of which I had completely ignored to date. I felt like I'd been set up!

Nobody apart from my mother knew anything about Kate at this point. I'd always kept all my cards very close to my chest, but even more so now I'd become a bit of a public figure. My business was my business and that was that. Knowing Kate would be calling soon, after she'd finished work, I made an excuse, grabbed a battery pack, and headed into Alness for a few hours to avoid my new roommate at all costs! I found a pub and ordered my usual cordial.

Like clockwork, Kate rang. She was always very sensitive about the fact I'd been walking all day and had limited battery and signal, so was good at keeping to her word when we arranged a time. After a catch-up, I told Kate about my situation back at Sam's place.

'You won't believe this, but a woman who hasn't left me alone on my page messenger is staying at the same house as I am! Her gear is all set up in the shed next to mine where I'm supposed to be sleeping. What am I going to do?'

Kate's reaction would be a gamechanger.

'Crikey, that does not sound ideal! Bunny boiler goes wild!' she laughed and, in the sweetest of voices, added: 'That is a bit weird though and, if I'm completely honest, I'd rather that didn't happen . . . but it's totally your call. If you feel okay with it then it's not my place to say at all, but, cards on the table, I can't say I'm totally comfortable with that being the situation.'

I nearly spat out my cordial! 'What do you mean?' I said, knowing full well what the answer was; I just really wanted to hear it.

'Well, I think it's pretty evident by now, Chris, that we may have stumbled over the friendship boundary, and I'm prepared to admit that I like you!'

With that, I slumped back in my chair with a grin you could have run a trainset across! *My god, she only bloody likes me! And not just as a friend!* I could have been attacked by ten men at that moment and I'd have just lain there and taken it, smiling all the while! Turns out my stalker had done me a favour! Now all I had to do was make my escape from the unwanted attention.

Now, with our feet and paws firmly on Black Isle, just about to hit our first city, Inverness, a lady called Sandra got in touch, offering Jet and me a barn to stay in while we completed this stretch of the coast. I loved the idea of having somewhere to come back to and get dry in now that the Scottish autumn was fully upon us. Sandra was so lovely and laid-back and would just leave Jet and me to it. I'm not exactly sure why, but Sandra was the first person, aside from my mother, that I told about Kate. Only a few days before, Kate had asked me if she could come up and visit me, and obviously, I agreed immediately. Sandra told me of a perfect place where we could have our first date; Eathie bothy, on the south side of the estuary that would take me to Inverness. She dropped me off to take a look. The place was a mess after some drunken youths had obviously partied there recently, so I decided to camp there for a few nights to spruce it up a bit. Plus, the idea of a little break, having walked non-stop from Wick by now, sounded good! So I spent a couple of days down the bottom of the cliffs nestled up inside the bothy and preparing it for our date. I made a brush from fern stalks and a piece of driftwood, lashed together with paracord I carried with me, swept the place out and gave it a once-over.

It was a small bothy and, unlike the ones I'd used on the west coast and the islands, easy to get to and probably visited regularly by walkers when the weather was good. For this reason, it had nothing inside except a very basic fireplace; it was just one bare room inside four stone walls with a door that no longer shut properly. In contrast, bothies on the west coast and islands are much more remote, frequented only by avid walkers, climbers and folks seeking adventure. They were full of lots of interesting artefacts (stag antlers, skulls, binoculars, candles) and littered with leftover food tins, but here there wasn't much need for them and, if I'm honest, anything worthwhile that was left would probably end up getting nicked so close to civilization! For the purpose of our date, however, it was just the ticket, and the best I was going to get where I knew we would be left alone.

6

The first date

For me, not being able to see Kate for six weeks was like somebody shutting the door and saying, 'Get to know each other before you meet again.' And it felt like the perfect foundation to build on. Still, the day Kate started making her way, first by train and then by air, to Inverness, I was a nervous wreck! What I did know was that the second Kate got there, it would be an immediate race to rush back to the bothy, as Jet and I had become finalists for a Soldiering On Award, and the virtual ceremony, which we'd already agreed to attend, was due to go live online an hour after she arrived.

At this point, it was October 2020, and events like this were all still taking place virtually rather than in person, due to ongoing Covid restrictions. That was fine with me – preferable in fact, as it saved me a long old trip to

London. Anyway, in the first hour of our first date, winning an award certainly wouldn't go against me, I thought!

Kate landed at Inverness and appeared from behind the sliding doors of the airport. Without a word spoken, we embraced, kissed, and cemented our mutual fondness for each other once and for all; it has to be one of the most wonderful moments of my life. We rushed back to Tug, a follower of my walk, who had kindly given me a lift to collect Kate, and raced back for the virtual award ceremony, all the while clutching hands and glancing excitedly at each other with beaming smiles. I cannot recall a moment in my life like it; I felt so happy. Kate was the one for me and I knew it.

Tug dropped us off at the edge of the woodland path that took us down to the bothy. With no time to lose, we just threw Kate's gear behind some bushes, and I asked Kate to follow on while Jet and I made a frantic sprint and scramble up to the top of a wooded, muddy hill, so we had sufficient signal to be able to log in to the Soldiering On Awards, which would start in just a few minutes. Jet and I had been nominated by the public and were finalists for the Animal Partnership Award. I'm not usually one for awards and big public accolades, but as awards go, the fact that this one was as much Jet's as it was mine meant a huge deal to me. What she had done for me and with me up to this point was so extraordinary, and it made my heart sing that she was being recognized for that.

It had been a race against time – so much so that on our first date I'd had to leave Kate on her own and just hope she'd find us! Find us she did, however, and just in time to watch as Jet and I were announced as the winners! I was delighted, as was Kate. I remember having a private chuckle to myself: 'Mate, you nailed the first kiss; before the second kiss you even won an award; and now you are going to teach her how to make a real fire, throw knives and forage for our own food. You total fucking stud!'

The next few days in Eathie bothy were just perfect. I was amazed at how enthusiastically Kate got stuck into my day-to-day tasks of finding and chopping wood, sourcing water, and keeping all our kit clean and dry. Better still, I could tell it wasn't just a front, but that she genuinely loved doing it. Each day, we would search for fallen logs and kindling to collect and chop for firewood, trek the few-miles round trip to the nearest farmhouse to collect water from their outside tap, search for fossils on the rocks, go crazy with our cameras taking photos of this beautiful spot we called home for three nights, and cook dinner over the fires we'd made. I was having the time of my life with her, and it was a lovely distraction from the constant focus needed daily to keep going on the walk.

By nightfall, the dark, cold bothy was aglow with light and warmth from a blazing fire we'd got going in the stone fireplace. Kate handed me a second glass of port she'd brought back for me from a recent surfing holiday in Portugal, and a song by Justin Vernon from Bon Iver came on, so we had a dance. Kate looked up at me with the most intensely beautiful eyes, and there was a little tear running down the side of her face.

'Chris,' she said in a soft, quiet voice. 'I think I'm in love with you.' It was the most perfect news to hear as I knew that I was already head over heels in love with her. This walk had not only helped to rebuild my life, but now it was also giving me everything I'd ever wanted, and it had all happened organically, by pure chance. You can spend your life looking for love, but ultimately it came and tapped me on the shoulder of its own accord.

We spent four days in and around the bothy, at which point our bubble burst as Kate had to return back to her mum's in Malvern to prep for Afghanistan, while I continued forth to Inverness.

I know I have spoken about the perks of being in cities, and don't get me wrong, it really was nice to have more shops around, but I'd forgotten the luxury and freedom of simple things – like being able to go for a piss anywhere, or even a number two for that matter! I can promise you it's not easy with my house and worldly possessions on my back, which I couldn't afford to ever let out of my sight, dressed in a kilt that inevitably soaks up the saturated floor of a public toilet, while a 28-kilo lurcher sits panting in my face, giving me no space to wipe my own arse! It was a disaster, and to make matters harder, every single time I ventured into a city, camping was off the cards. I didn't mind sleeping rough in cities, and I had many a time, but give me the option of a wild mountainside or a piss-ridden doorway and it's not hard to guess which I'd choose.

Coming into a city after years of traipsing through little hamlets dotted around and mostly wild, untouched coastline was more of a shock than I'd imagined. The first thing I noticed was the noise! City life was simply the wrong kind of noise for me. It was never right for me before, but now the feeling was far more intense. Whether it was because my hearing had improved or just the fact that I'd spent practically every night in complete silence with only the sounds of birds, or the occasional badger or fox rustling for any sign of food I may have spilt while cooking, I wasn't sure, but both Jet and I near jumped out of our skin whenever a bus passed by! My god, it was deafening. As we made our way into the city centre, I had to put Jet on a lead, and she goes into a 'sod you' mode when I do that, and would plod along so slowly. It frustrated me, but what could I do?

To my sheer delight, a lovely follower called Shoenag reached out and offered me a back garden in which to pitch my tent, as well as a warm meal – perfect! Shoenag was your typical chatty, bubbly, caring Scottish woman in her late fifties/early sixties. Like so many other Scots I'd met, there just wasn't enough she could do for me! More than anything, she was a joy to be around. I stayed for a couple of nights to recharge my battery packs and wash all my gear ready to hit our next stretch of coast.

The night before leaving Shoenag's, I said my goodbyes to Kate over the phone. In the early hours of the following morning, she was heading to Afghanistan for two weeks. If I'm honest, I had mixed emotions about her going. I'd never have told her not to, it wasn't my place, but as an ex-Para it was not a place I associated with being a great holiday destination. To give Kate her dues, she was going with more in mind than just a holiday. She had been in touch with some Italian philanthropists who had opened several schools in the province of Bamiyan, which she planned to visit in the hope she might be able to launch a project training teachers out there to improve educational access and outcomes, particularly for girls.

Kate was so passionate about her work and so determined to make a difference; she had big dreams, incredible vision and worked seriously hard. It really was inspiring to listen to. More than anything, she wanted to make a positive difference in people's lives, particularly children and those in less fortunate circumstances – so much so that she was willing to head to a war zone to do it. She was also going hiking in the mountains and wanted to see the country from another perspective, uncover a different narrative other than the one-sided war-torn view depicted all the time in the media. As she was an adventurer herself, I got the sense that the thrill of exploring a land that us Westerners knew so little of had real appeal for her, a land that was essentially off-limits.

I had to give it to her: she had real guts. I had so much admiration for her in many ways, but at the same time it didn't sit comfortably with me at all. I mean this with absolutely no disrespect to the people of Afghanistan, but, as I had lost good friends there and given that the country was still far from settled, her being there gave me real anxiety. I understood the daring, adventurous, risk-taking side of it, I really did, but the cynical, untrusting side of me had crept its way in, despite Kate's best efforts to persuade me that she was in good hands. She wasn't going alone, at least, and would be travelling with a company that specialized in taking very small groups of experienced, open-minded travellers to countries that were perceived to be off-limits to foreigners. Every precaution was being made to ensure they would be kept safe, but it still didn't make me feel any better. Regardless of the fact that Kate was experienced, the region was volatile and I simply saw it as a case of wrong place, wrong time.

I felt like I'd just met the woman of my dreams. At forty years old, I'd finally found the one for me, the woman I wanted to be with. For so long, I thought she didn't exist, and love just wasn't on the cards for me. My mind was racing with all the what-ifs. What if something happened to her out there? What if she needed help and I couldn't be there to protect her? How cruel it would be to find my perfect woman only to have her ripped from me under circumstances that could so easily have been avoided! If anything happened to Kate out there, I would be devastated. The thought of it was unbearable.

That night, in a bid for positive distraction, I decided to make it public on my page that I'd met someone. The response was just incredible – a real testament to the love and support I had gained across all four corners of the UK and beyond. My followers were genuinely happy for me; to have started as a broken shell of a man and over the years to have grown as I had in front of everybody's eyes, adopting a beautiful dog who became my loyal, devoted companion and then to have found love – this adventure had now turned into something beautiful, and had captured the attention of so many. Compared to so much negativity going on in the world, it was a positive story of hope, transformation, finding happiness – and now love.

7

Lunch in the Officers' Mess

The next few days, I worked my way from Inverness to Fort George. The coastline itself was so much flatter than anything I'd seen in a long time, as slowly but surely the land was becoming more agricultural – barbed-wire fences causing us all sorts of problems, especially Jet. The coastline was stitched in fences, which involved climbing over one for every field I crossed. At 28 kilos, lifting Jet single-handedly over the barbed wire was no easy feat. It was fine lifting her over the top, but putting her down meant leaning over the wire mid-chest. I always wrapped my coat around the section of barbed wire I'd lean over, but, no matter how secure the coat was, mine and Jet's weight proved too much.

Every time, the barbed wire pierced through my jacket and continually stabbed me in the chest. And it hurt!

Often, I would get angry with myself, with loads of little stab holes in my chest (I still bear the scars to this day) and a kilt that was becoming more and more tattered with rips as I went on, knowing only a few hundred yards away was the easy option of the road! It was like this, though – more than just a target or a goal, I'd made a pact with myself from the beginning to stick as rigidly as humanly possible to the actual coastline, bar the odd power station or military firing range, and by now, it had become an obsession. I'd just completed the west coast of Scotland and all its islands and kept going through their blistering winters, so I'd often remind myself that I had nothing to prove to anyone, not even to myself for that matter. But it didn't make a difference – I knew deep down that I couldn't claim to have walked the entire UK coastline if I took short cuts or the easier option from time to time when the going got tough. It just isn't in my blood.

The first and next two military camps, Fort George and Lossiemouth, really made a wonderfully big deal of my arrival. Fort George was amazing. The camp itself is an eighteenth-century fortress near Ardersier, northeast of Inverness, on a promontory sticking out into the Moray Firth. It's an incredible feat of engineering, stretching back to suppress the Jacobite ambitions after the famous nearby Battle of Culloden up until now, where it stands as a base for the Scottish Black Watch. Although the fort has never once fired a single shot in anger, its location on the firth means it holds a prime defensive position against any potential invasion to this day.

I was given a room to shower in and rest, after which the CO (Commanding Officer) invited me for lunch up in the Officers' Mess. The whole battalion had come out onto the square to parade and to take a photo with Jet and me standing in front. It really was such a lovely welcome – no camp up until this point had even invited me in, let alone pulled out all the stops! It was a lovely reminder that, once upon a time, I had been part of something unique and special. I felt warm inside leaving Fort George, a sense of brothers-in-arms and that once you had been part of it you would carry that torch for ever.

I'd managed to have a few brief video calls with Kate while she was away in Afghanistan, more so because she understood that I was keen for a heads-up every now and then to make sure she was okay, but on her last day, when I knew she was back in Kabul preparing to transfer to the airport for her flight home, I received a message. She told me a bomb had gone off in the capital and they were being taken to a safe house as a security measure while they waited for their Covid tests to come back to make sure they could fly. My heart sunk. I must have gone white in that moment. I kept sending messages through but none of them were being delivered. Kate obviously had her own problems to deal with out there and I could only assume that the frantic nature of the situation meant that she was on the move or out of signal.

For the next nine hours, I didn't hear a single thing. I felt sick the entire time. For that whole day walking, I pushed myself so hard physically just to try to take my mind off it, but with little success. I was beside myself, with no way to make contact, no control over the situation and no way to hear a thing.

After hours of torturing myself with all of the what-ifs and the feeling of utter helplessness, I finally received a message from Kate to say it had been impossible to message from Kabul but she had arrived safely at Dubai airport. She also told me she had decided to get a flight straight from Heathrow airport up to me in Inverness rather than head home to her mum's in Malvern. I was so relieved, and over the moon knowing I'd be seeing her again in just two days! After living with my heart in my throat every day for two weeks, knowing that she was returning in one piece and that she wasn't wasting any time in coming to see me was just the peace of mind I needed. I couldn't wait.

By the time Kate arrived back in Inverness, a lady called Nikki had reached out offering me a wooden annex in her back garden in Balloch, which belonged to her mum. Nikki was so excited for me that Kate was coming up and offered us the use of the annex for a good week or so, giving us loads of space and time to hang out on our own. I loved having Kate around; it was only our second date really, the third time we'd ever even seen each other in person, but as her time with me neared the end, it was obvious that neither of us wanted to stay apart, not for one second! Then, one morning, she just came out with it.

'Chris, what if I came and joined you for the rest of the walk?'

I just smiled and that was that. I didn't even need to

think twice. I'd been alone with Jet on this walk for so long that it was all I knew, and, in many ways, I was perfectly happy with that. I had never once even consider-ed the prospect of it being any other way, but as soon as the words left her mouth, I just knew the answer was yes. The more I thought about it over the coming days, I wondered if she had any idea what she was getting herself into. This was a girl who was used to the London life and the comforts of a warm bed and a well-heated house. And here she was, in November, about to join a walk that involved living outside and all the serious hard-ships that entailed, and she'd yet to even walk a day of it with me. Yes, we'd spent those few days in Eathie bothy, but we weren't moving on day to day, as was my usual life, and that was mid-October. She was about to dive headfirst into a Scottish winter on the east coast without even having sampled a proper taste of life on this walk. Then there were the ins and outs of leaving her job and handing over work commitments that needed sorting. At that moment, however, none of that mattered. I beamed from ear to ear. Kate was all in.

It was a massive decision for her. She wasn't coming from nothing, with nothing to lose like I had; she had a fantastic, extremely successful career that she had spent the past ten years building. She had *everything* to lose. But, when push came to shove, she was willing to follow her heart and give up everything she knew at the drop of a hat because it felt right. She wasn't afraid to grab the bull by the horns in life and, my god, I loved her for it.

Kate's first experience of the walk would take us to

Lossiemouth, an RAF camp a little further south from Fort George, which was much bigger and armed with some incredible flying machines. The reception when we arrived was mind-blowing. A squad came to meet us on the beach and escorted us for about half a mile from the coast up through the village to the base. Hordes of villagers, including the local primary school, lined the pavements waving banners of support, clapping and cheering us on, with people coming over to hand us gifts, including a new handmade winter coat for Jet, as well as press interviewing me as I walked.

Once we made it to the entrance of the base, we were then greeted by the commanding officer, who personally escorted me in a very exclusive car to HQ. It was insane. When Kate met me, she'd heard nothing about me or the walk. Even at this point, she really had no idea what the walk was like or how popular it was becoming. Having only just joined, she was still unknown and certainly not perceived as a member of the pack just yet. As I've always said, respect is earned, not given. Kate knew this and she still had to earn hers. I still find it funny to this day that when I got into the CO's blacked-out car with Jet, being treated like royalty, Kate was mugged off and asked to walk and meet us there! My dry sense of humour found this incredibly amusing. I didn't tell her then, but even I was astonished at the welcome we received, and I know Kate was too.

With all the little signs I'd learned to read weather-wise over the past three years living outside, I could tell that soon enough a cold snap was inevitable at any time. I got to work fixing and mending any bits of kit that needed it in preparation for winter. Kate needed a massive upgrade on her gear if she had any hope of surviving winter up here, especially given the fact that she felt the cold easily. Fortunately, she had some savings from a big project she'd led over lockdown, making educational videos for teachers and parents that had been distributed nationally to support home learning, and, with my advice, used that to get most of what she needed. The only thing she was still lacking was a decent sleeping bag. She'd got a new jacket at least, just in time.

Having another human with me was a real joy, but I suddenly felt a huge sense of added responsibility. Jet was a seasoned walker and, especially now we were on the east coast, I felt very little concern for her given her experience and fitness. I had every faith there was nothing to worry about with Jet, but with Kate it was different.

I find it hard to imagine what must have gone through Kate's parents' minds when they found out their daughter had just given up an outstanding ten-year career earning good money (certainly by my standards) to go and sleep in a tent with a hairy, totally skint homeless man and his dog! This is a girl who'd spent five years studying at St Andrews (where Prince William and Kate Middleton met, no less), a far cry from having walked out of GCSEs at sixteen like me. She was giving it all up and, since her parents had never heard of or met me, any concerns on their part were understandable, I suppose. Kate's ability to act on a gut feeling and take a massive chance with the risk of losing it all is a world away from her parents, who have a more traditional mindset. It's something deeply rooted and unique in her. However, I knew by now that this is the kind of quality that can make people go far in life. We are both like it and we thrive on it. It's what I like to call healthy gambling. To me, it seems like a very dull existence to float through life never taking any big chances – where's the fun in that?

Regardless of the fact that Kate's travel track record showed she could take care of herself, she still had a lot to learn, especially when it came to the survival aspect. Nomadic life in the great outdoors means constant risk assessments, always looking ahead, scouting the land as you walk for escape routes in case of emergency, understanding weather systems as well as fire, foraging and, of course, harnessing the land and sea, whether it be for food, firewood or safe spots to camp. The list goes on. It takes years of doing it constantly every day and honing your craft to even think about calling yourself a pro.

Kate was incredibly keen to learn and so hands-on; she wasn't fazed by hard graft or getting her hands dirty, and she'd made it very clear to me that now she'd joined this walk, she wasn't just 'along for the ride'; she wanted it to be a 50:50 team effort when it came to all the chores and demands of living outside. She knew she had a lot to absorb and, having spent so long doing it all on my own, it gave me a lot of pleasure to be able to teach her the knowledge I'd gained along the way, most of it from my mistakes! Being shown how to do something by someone is far less of an effective learning curve than having to work it out for yourself. Never before on the journey had I had someone to share everything I knew about survival with, and I took great pride in teaching Kate what I believe is a long-lost art in the Western world.

Kate had settled into the walk nicely as we made our way down the coast towards Aberdeen through Banff, Macduff, Fraserburgh and Peterhead. We fell in love with the small fishing villages we passed through along the way, particularly Pennan, Gardenstown and Rosehearty. They were like some of those we passed on the southwest of England, but the major difference being that they were far less busy and the beautiful sea-facing fishing cottages were still occupied by locals rather than serving as summer retreats for wealthy Londoners who might use them only a few months or even weeks of the year. It gave a much warmer feel and the communities were more tight-knit, the locals so friendly and welcoming, often giving us donations as we passed through, and not just for the charity but for our survival fund to help us keep going.

Not a single hamlet or village didn't reach out to offer help if it was needed. It deepened my belief that people up north and beyond the English border into Scotland are so much warmer in character compared with anywhere else I'd lived in the UK. Even Kate noticed the difference straight away. People offering sheds, garages, even the occasional small boat in the harbour – which I can tell you is immense fun in a storm, as we experienced one very rocky night in Peterhead about 20 miles north of Aberdeen.

With winter now firmly set in and Christmas just around the corner, we decided that we would spend Christmas Eve sleeping rough on the streets of Aberdeen to raise awareness for the homeless. It was something I'd planned to do way before meeting Kate, as I had done this regularly in cities throughout my walk to date. I felt really strongly about raising the profile for the homeless on this walk.

I was currently homeless myself, and if I'm honest I had been several times before in my past, but the big difference now was that I had the most important thing of all: a purpose and a clear goal in life. That didn't mean that I didn't get lonely or feel vulnerable at times. Though, granted, my vulnerabilities were more the fear of raging wind, falling rocks or breaking the occasional bone (or even teeth for that matter!). A real sense of self-worth had regenerated over the past few years, which made the feeling of essentially being homeless completely different, but I'd been there, and I have and always will have a deep, deep empathy for anyone sleeping rough as a last resort.

When I told Kate about the plan to sleep rough in the cities we passed through, she thought it was a great idea. Having lived in London for ten years and travelled widely, Kate had seen her fair share of homelessness as well. Although our backgrounds couldn't have been more different (Kate had certainly never even come close to facing homelessness herself), she was always eager to do what she could to help others. That was something that had been very apparent since we'd first started getting to know each other, and probably the reason she became a teacher in the first place. My admiration for her 'let's go for it' mentality was growing stronger by the day. What a woman!

8

Christmas with Aberdeen's homeless

One thing that really struck me, and that I noticed more and more on the east coast as winter set in, was the drop in temperature. The difference between winter on the east and west coasts is noteworthy. The warmer Atlantic currents and the mountainous terrain of the west mean that the Western Highlands have more rainfall than anywhere else in the UK. It also means that the weather is far more unpredictable and, in my experience, brutal. The east coast on the other hand is affected by the colder North Sea currents, which, combined with less mountainous terrain and much flatter land, makes winter temperatures considerably colder – and we were about to experience the coldest up here in thirty-two years.

Our first real experience of this just happened to be on Christmas Eve, when we decided to sleep rough for the evening in the city centre of Aberdeen, underneath the bandstand in St George's Square. I must admit that I had some real reservations about doing this, not so much because we were going to be sleeping rough on a very cold night in the minuses without the protection of our tent, or even the fact that it might unravel some difficult past experiences, bringing up unwanted feelings that I hoped I would never have to encounter again, but because sleeping in the middle of the city is completely different to sleeping out in the wilds.

I felt so much safer being in the middle of nowhere on my own in the tent than exposed under the bandstand, like a tortoise without his shell. In my tent I was in full control, and as I've always said on this journey to anybody that asked, when camping, the more people that you are around, the more dangerous it becomes. It only takes one fool to ruin everything, and what could've been a wonderful experience to raise some extra money for charity and to help highlight homelessness could turn on a sixpence into an utter nightmare.

Deep down, I also knew that I now had the added responsibility of making sure that Kate got through the night safely. And while I felt sure I'd be able to look after myself if any unwanted trouble came my way, I wasn't sure I'd be able to look after myself, my dog and my girlfriend all at the same time. Kate's parents knew what we were doing and would have had reservations about her safety, so I made a pact to myself that I would stay up the entire night to keep guard and make sure that I could look after my little family unit the best I could.

Kate being Kate was as ever up for the challenge as we walked into Aberdeen. For her, this would be a whole new experience, a great little adventure as well as affording a more in-depth insight into what it must be like for people who, I know, Kate has often stopped for in the past to give the odd fiver or some food that she had just brought on her lunch break from work back in London. It would be interesting to get Kate's perspective on what it felt like to be on the other side for a change. However, both she and I knew that we were in a very different position to those who were sleeping out. For a start, we had the love and support of people all around the UK who were aware what we were doing as well as the security of knowing that if ever we needed it, a simple ask or shout-out on social media would bring people rushing to our aid. We also knew that the following evening we would be snuggled into our sleeping bags somewhere on the coast in our little orange bubble, getting ready for the next day, fully in control of what we were doing. And of course, there was the one thing we had that they didn't – the all-important *purpose* in life. A place to head to.

As we laid our sleeping bags on the bandstand floor and got Jet nice and cosy ready for the evening, Aberdeen was still thriving and buzzing with people. I knew what was to come, something that is hard to explain if you have never been sleeping rough on the streets before. As night time closes in and the constant sound of people going about their city life starts to recede as one by one each person retreats to their home, it's at this point you really start to realize that you are all on your own in a cold,

71

uncaring concrete jungle. I can honestly say it's a very eerie silence once the streets have emptied – but that is a presumption, because not everybody is now happily tucked away in their beds getting a great night's sleep. There are always nocturnal predators to be vigilant of.

It's one thing to be homeless and sofa-surfing at a friend's place or even with a family member, as I had also done many times in the past, but it's quite another to find yourself living rough on the streets. After a while, doing it for weeks on end, it starts to destroy your soul – something I can relate to wholeheartedly. You feel dirty, weak from malnutrition, and of course there's that ever-prodding feeling of utter self-worthlessness. This feeling of having failed in society is reinforced by the expressions of nine out of ten people who walk past you and pretend you're not there.

So many homeless that take to the streets end up abusing alcohol and other drugs simply as a way to mingle with others who can relate to them, and for that short time with whatever substance they've chosen to help them get through the evening, they feel at least a little bit happy before it all happens again the next day. Sadly, this daily routine can turn into weeks, weeks turn into months and often into years. Before long it becomes the norm, and some homeless individuals genuinely believe they have a happier life living rough on the streets and even choose to continue doing so. I can understand that would be hard to fathom for a lot of people having never been in a situation that has driven them to make these life choices, I really do.

In a world with mental health issues now at the forefront of so many conversations, it completely baffles me to the point of anger how we can be so blasé about these poor souls who have absolutely nothing, when so many have so much. I will simply never understand how we can consider these people a nuisance rather than a priority. It's reasons like this that made me lose my faith in humanity before I started this walk, having once been one of those troubled persons myself.

The bandstand we'd chosen proved a well-located spot for us to cross paths with some of the homeless in Aberdeen. As Christmas Eve turned into the early hours of Christmas morning, the streets were now completely silent and empty apart from the occasional homeless person who would walk past and either offer or ask us for drugs or alcohol. I kept a very close watch on who approached us. At around 2 a.m., the heavens suddenly opened and gave us a spectacular display; for the first time for as long as I can remember, it snowed on Christmas Eve! A slight easterly wind pushed the snow beneath the bandstand where Kate and I lay, covering our sleeping bags as they became wetter and wetter by the hour. It was uncomfortable to say the least. However, there was something to be said about being in the centre of Aberdeen, both staying awake the entire evening with Jet nestled in between us and happily snoring away to welcome in Christmas.

We felt pleased we'd decided to highlight homelessness on an evening when so many went to bed excited to wake up on Christmas Day surrounded by love and warmth, in a cosy house, celebrating with their families and opening presents around a magical Christmas tree. Now with around 80,000 followers on my social media, it felt only right to use this platform to try to do something positive for those less fortunate. It was astonishing to see others staying out late on nights that could have been spent with their families, pushing around food carts armed with teas, coffees and blankets for the homeless. It is incredibly heart-warming to know there's so many good, selfless kind souls who genuinely care.

I sat in silence, watching these individuals quietly going about their philanthropy, wondering why on earth so many celebrities get awards for basically doing nothing or just for being famous. These people in the freezing cold, doing their bit for humanity without a single thought for themselves, or need for any kind of praise, they were the true heroes, the ones who deserved medals.

As the sun started to rise and with the coldest part of the night now behind us, Kate and I were still awake cuddled up together in our sleeping bags for warmth, when some early-morning visitors appeared. They'd watched the posts I'd put out on my page overnight and had come to offer us coffee and any help if needed. It was so lovely and so appreciated; we could only hope that others sleeping rough were getting the same treatment. It had been a cold night on the insanely hard floor of the bandstand, so we decided to get up and, to help us warm up, walk down to the coastline. To say we were tired is an understatement. Kate and I both commented on how stiff our bodies had become from lying on the cold concrete floor. We needed to get moving to warm up the muscles and feel some kind of normality. To our astonishment and pure joy, we were welcomed onto the coast with possibly one of the best sunrises we had ever seen. The thin overcast cloud cover riddled with small holes allowed a glimpse to clear skies and made for a magnificent display of purples, reds and blues. Kate, Jet and I just stared in pure silence and marvelled at such a gift from Mother Nature; it was the perfect way to see in Christmas morning. I think it's safe to say that in the serenity of the sunrise, we totally forgot how cold we were and had been for the past twelve hours.

9

Keeping busy in lockdown

Lockdown number two was just around the corner, starting on Boxing Day, but, unlike the first mandatory order to stay at home, we had a bit of time on our hands to search for a spot to set up camp. We looked high and low – inside a castle ruin, even going so far as to contemplate staying in an underground bunker once used in World War Two. However, the bunker was completely impractical given how damp and dark it was inside, never mind the ladder access underground, which would've meant precariously getting Jet up and down without a hint of a slip. It took a good deal of poring over the map, but eventually we found somewhere just south of Aberdeen. It would mean jumping forward slightly on our walk, but once this lockdown was over, we would simply return to where we'd left off at Slains Castle in Aberdeenshire.

We decided that a patch of woodland between the small villages of Gourdon and Johnshaven would be just the ticket. The woodland was much longer than it was wide and only a few hundred yards from the coastline, which meant we felt like we were still staying true to the nature of the walk by being right next to the coast. We had phone signal there and the location between villages meant we had access to a village shop about a mile's walk away for supplies, which was imperative. The tiny village shops were being kept open during the lockdown as a necessity for the community, and there was also a Co-op, as well as a food bank in the slightly further town of Inverbervie, which we could walk to as well. The woodland was cut off by fields occupied with sheep kept in by an old stone wall that ran along a coastal path. We would then pass through a small gate and walk through a field to get up onto the track that eventually took us to our chosen spot. Given how long we might be there, the walk to get supplies would turn out to be a refreshing change, and a welcome escape.

I knew from the previous lockdown experience that the only way that we would get through this, especially in the height of winter, would be to keep ourselves incredibly busy. We both discussed and agreed that we would do whatever it took to keep ourselves warm and always occupied so as not to dampen our morale by becoming bored and restless. In a way, the eastern cold front that was undoubtedly going to hit us also served as a favour. The cold would give us added incentive to keep busy at all times until we were tucked up inside our orange bubble, ready to hit the sack.

Once again, I found myself in complete awe of Kate's incredibly positive attitude, lust for adventure and ability to take whatever was thrown her way as an opportunity to learn. I really don't know many people who could've quite easily gone to a nice warm home back in Malvern for the entire lockdown and yet chose to spend the winter in the northeast of Scotland where we would inevitably be freezing cold the entire time with no more than £50 to our name and nothing but uncertainty as to how things would pan out. In fact, I sensed a real excitement in her at the challenge, and just knew that I had found someone incredibly special. I really don't think that I had ever admired and felt such a kindred spirit with anybody so much in my entire life.

What had made things extra special was watching the growing bond between my two beautiful girls, Jet and Kate. Fortunately for me, Kate loved dogs and had fallen in love with Jet from the word go. Don't get me wrong: Jet was and will always be a one-man dog; where I go she goes, but it was clear to see that Kate had completely earned Jet's trust and love. At night times, Jet would nestle in between Kate and me to keep warm and now received double the amount of attention that she did before. Each evening, she would get double tickles from both mine and Kate's direction. You could see the happiness and contentment in her face. I'd already told Kate, and this may sound crazy to any non-dog lovers, that it would never work out between us if Jet had not accepted Kate the way she had, but fortunately, the mutual bond was clear to see. Thank God for that!

The woodland that we had chosen was situated pretty much at the bottom of a very gradual but long hill, meaning the woods themselves during autumn (or the wet season as I called it) would be swamped with water running down it constantly. The wet ground meant the trees were unable to hold their roots and each year, without a doubt, they would fall, giving us an abundance of firewood: an absolute must for us if we were to stay there for the duration of lockdown over winter. With very little money, we were unable to sustain ourselves alone on foraged firewood without needing gas to cook. We would need to build a Dakota-style oven under the ground as well as fire pits to hang pots, enabling us to cook in all weathers. Once our basic camp was set up, I got busy creating fire pits and stoves with Kate always by my side, asking questions and learning as we went. It was an absolute joy to teach such a keen student.

As we were exhausted from Christmas Eve on the streets, it was really too late in the day to cook our bush-craft Christmas dinner outdoors by the time we got back to the woods, and we still needed to polish off our camp set-up, but we were determined to have our Christmas dinner irrespective. Thanks to the good people of Gourdon and Inverbervie, we were blessed with a chicken and all the trimmings for a wonderful dinner on Christmas Day. It would be the first time in my entire life that I had the challenge of making a full roast dinner utilizing what little we had around us to cook. Even Christmas dinner at home in an oven is not the easiest of tasks, but we loved the idea of the challenge and for the first time used our

Dakota oven to cook the chicken on a spit over a fire pit that we had already dug!

The biggest challenge would be the roast potatoes and stuffing, but we were up for it and, regardless of how it tasted, it would've been a monumental feat for us. We got to work in the morning using a bag of coal that was given to us for the fire pit and making a fire out of fallen wood for the Dakota oven. At this time of year, it was already dark by around 3.30 p.m., meaning we ended up cooking in darkness, which I can promise you is not an easy task. We only had our head torches, and it was so dark at night in the woods with no ambient light to give any aid, which made everything very tricky!

The hardest part, like any roast dinner, was making sure that the timing was perfect. The chicken, potatoes, stuffing and roasted vegetables, which I'd never cooked this way before, needed to all be ready at the same time if dinner was to be in any way warm, as there was no microwave to reheat! After a huge effort, and in total darkness, Kate and I sat down on top of our bags to feast on our efforts with some plastic plates and a glass of bubbly. It wasn't the best Christmas dinner I've ever eaten, but it was without a doubt the most satisfying, given that we'd spent all day cooking it.

It was so much fun. Kate had spent the evening before creating an after-dinner game for us to play by head torch – her own twist on Snakes and Ladders created by pen on an old piece of roll mat. She'd even made Christmas hats for us out of paper and some clip-on baubles she'd somehow managed to get hold of to decorate my beard as a joke! It was mine and Kate's first Christmas together and we had a wonderful time. Jet got a huge share of the chicken and other bits and bobs, and she went to sleep a very happy and full dog. In all, it was a wonderful experience.

A few days into lockdown, Kate and I decided to divide and conquer the woodland, delving in different directions to go and collect firewood for the evening ready to get a fire bursting with warmth before the night closed in. It was part of our daily routine that we set up to keep us active and warm. Living outdoors in harsh and unpredictable weather conditions means having to plan ahead all of the time; a mistake or forgetting something like enough firewood would mean we would pay the price later, so we were on it constantly, and always ready for whatever the weather threw at us.

Next to the tent was a big fallen-down tree that I guessed had been there around a year. The wood was still strong and relatively fresh, and at some point someone (I assume families with children) had laid thinner branches up against it to make a small base. The huge tree trunk had two branches around a foot thick that stuck out in different directions, much like a fork without the inner prongs. You could stand in between these with plenty of space and it was just above head height. As I stood inside, I shouted over to Kate, 'Mate, this would be a perfect place to build a home to shelter us when it rains. And we could even stand up in it rather than just sitting inside the tent!'

With her eyes beaming, Kate looked back at me and said, 'Great idea. Let's do it; we can start now!'

'That's my girl!'

I knew of a technique called 'cobb walling', which was used thousands of years ago by our ancestors to build huts for families that were strong, sturdy, waterproof, windproof and simple to make if you didn't mind a good graft and getting your hands dirty! We would have to collect a ridiculous number of logs as long and as thick as possible to build the outer and inner walls. To bond it together, our ancestors would use a combination of cowpat, small stones and mud that, when dried, acts exactly like cement.

We didn't have the luxury of cow shit, and seeing as we knew the shelter was only going to be a temporary fix for us, it didn't matter. So long as we used good rope to tie the wooden walls together and packed in between the inner and outer walls solidly with stone and mud, I knew it would serve its purpose perfectly. We got to work immediately.

Along with all the other chores: collecting water and firewood, getting supplies, cleaning our cooking pots and disposing of rubbish or unwanted food so as not to attract rats, birds, foxes or badgers, our new project was a wonderful way to keep the mind active and the body moving, and to stop the bitter winter cold creeping into the bones. The wood alone took weeks of constant scouring up and down the woods, scavenging anything that we thought could be useful. It was hard work, and tedious if I'm honest, as pickings were slim. As we started to build the walls from the ground up, however, and we saw signs of some kind of structure taking shape, we really began to get excited and worked tirelessly day and night, often well into the evening to get it built as soon as possible.

Seeing as it was only a temporary shelter, Kate and I would only collect or chop wood from trees that had already fallen, using an axe that I borrowed from a local. I would lay a length of wood on the floor with an adjacent piece of wood about a foot apart, and fill the space in between with a mix of soil and stone. I would then hammer smaller pieces of wood or splints either side of each length to make sure they were solidly in place and didn't move. After, we would pack stone and mud as compactly as we possibly could in between the two lengths until it reached the top of each piece of wood. Then we'd lay another two logs on top of the section just completed, bind them together with rope so they were completely solid, and repeat the process, building up and up until eventually they met with the branches of the tree that had fallen, essentially acting as rolled steel joists. It was a relentless process and, with only the winter sea to wash our hands and faces from the constant hammering down of the mud and stone, both Kate and I would go to bed looking like we'd just spent a week down a coal mine. But we didn't care. Slowly but surely, day after day, our shelter was start-ing to emerge. We would take turns to go foraging for fallen logs of the correct length in the woods while the other packed the mud and continued building the walls up. Jet would just sit and watch wondering what the hell we were doing and was just happy not to be moving, always snuggled up cosily in a sleeping bag. She is a true hound, shivers within seconds and genuinely doesn't like the cold, so it goes without saying that making sure she was toasty was a priority before we did anything else.

To break up the constant routine of collecting logs, stacking one log on top of the other, fastening it with ropes and then packing it with mud and stone, Kate and I devised little ways to instil a bit more fun into day-to-day life. Just really simple things like throwing a frisbee or playing catch with a tennis ball, always some way to keep our fitness levels up. Part of the rules we concocted were that if you missed the frisbee or the ball, you'd have to do push-ups and sit-ups as penalties. Given the fact that her frisbee skills and catching skills were in no way, shape or form up to my standards, Kate would inevitably end up doing double the number of press-ups and sit-ups as me. She did so many, I began to feel sorry for her, but I will admit that the sadistic side of me did enjoy it, and I knew it would only benefit her on a fitness front, getting her ready for when we would set off once again. I would just laugh and tell her to get on with it!

We also used the field just below the woods as a training ground, where we would run laps, especially on particularly cold days, to keep warm and get fitter. Just like the first lockdown on Hildasay, when I'd promised myself I would benefit somehow from the time stuck in one spot alone and use it to better serve me rather than let it get me down, this is exactly the same approach we adopted for lockdown number two.

To my delight, only a few weeks before lockdown kicked in, I'd received a call from my friend and producer Tim, who got in touch back in Shetland about the possibility of filming a documentary for BBC Wales. Tim gave me the good news that his pitch had been put forward to BBC London, who had given the go-ahead to film a documentary that would be shared across the entire UK. I was so happy. I really believed that all my efforts so far deserved this, and I knew it would help boost the donations. Since my first discussion with Tim, the whole story had gained more and more interest and evolved dramatically. What was initially a story about a broken man who set out to walk the entire UK coastline and raise money for charity had turned into an unexpected love story now that Kate was on the scene. Even better, it just so happened that Kate was a complete natural in front of a camera, which I'd quickly realized after we'd both been interviewed for various news channels as we passed through each county. Kate and I would both enjoy getting our story out.

After a month of solid graft, working all day and into the nights, we finally finished our woodland home. In all, it was about 70 feet long by 7 feet wide at its most spacious point inside, with a smaller compartment at the back to store supplies rather than them taking room up in the tent. The wooden walls were around a foot thick all the way around the shelter, offering us ample protection from any big winds that would come our way. Thanks to some locals, we borrowed two big tarps that we fastened together as a roof over the shelter to keep out any rain. Having seen the technique myself in Viking houses back in Shetland as well as Black Houses in the

Outer Hebrides, we got to work digging a fire pit in the centre of our shelter and I devised a way to move the tarps to one side, creating a gap in our makeshift roof to allow any smoke to funnel out of rather than choking us to death inside. We would use this fire for heat and for cooking if the weather was so miserable and wet that we were unable to use the fire pits we had dug outside. As homes go, it was as basic as they come, but we were delighted with it, even more so given we had built it by hand ourselves. The nights of being cramped, sitting hunched over and squashed in the tent were no more. With Jet tucked up in the sleeping bag inside the wooden structure next to us, Kate and I sat around the fire while some strategically placed candles gave us some atmospheric light. I think it's safe to say we had achieved what we set out to, learning as we went. It really was a wonderful feeling and worth every splinter we would spend the next few weeks pulling out of ourselves. It's all about the little wins.

10

Jet scare

Tim and his colleague Tom arrived at camp in early to mid-February ready to start filming the first instalment of the documentary. We had pre-warned them that the winter had turned bitterly cold, with temperatures dropping down to −17 degrees at night here just south of Aberdeen. So far, it had been the coldest winter the area had seen in over twenty-five years, with Storm Darcy bringing an unusually cold spell our way, including a load of snow. The night they arrived, we sat around our campfire under a black sky showered in droplets of snow. By morning, our camp, tent and wooden house were completely white as we got up to get the fire on to warm the bones and get breakfast cooking. Freezing as it was, we saw it as a positive when it came to filming – not only would it make for some stunning white backdrops, but it would help to really show the reality of what living outdoors through winter on this walk was like.

Having spent the past three years of the walk alone with Jet, as well as having been a single parent for ten years prior to setting off, it had become a deeply ingrained habit for me to keep myself and any problems I had all to myself. Given the difficult position that we were in, existing on our wits with no electricity or warmth on tap, I found people that whinged about what were first-world problems – like one of their appliances not working – incredibly hard to be around. I never really moaned about anything and just got on with it. This mentality also meant that I never asked for anything on the walk. However, sometimes this mentality can come back to bite you; for example, after finishing Shetland and spending the winter out there, my boots, which had lasted me all the way from the Outer Hebrides, had become riddled with holes and the soles had almost completely disintegrated. As a result, from the most northern point of mainland Scotland up until now, I had walked all of the coast in a pair of wetsuit boots that by this point had very little left holding them together. During the day when we were walking, the snow would seep in and surround my feet and then melt inside my wetsuit boots. Slowly but surely, my feet would become numb, and the pain would get worse and worse as the cold of the evening drew in. It was excruciating! Now that was a problem worth whingeing about.

The first day of filming, which consisted of shooting in certain locations that we'd already covered – doing take after take to make sure it was all perfect – didn't finish for me until late into the night. Tim was busy getting footage that showed me cooking and preparing for the evening; going down to the sea collecting salt water that could then be boiled for Kate's hot-water bottles. When I got into the tent ready to hit the sack, Kate could immediately tell something was up and asked me why I was in such a mood when she thought I'd be enjoying the experience of filming a documentary I'd been so excited about. I'm really not a fan of pity or people feeling sorry for me; normally I'd have just kept it to myself and lay in the sleeping bag as quiet as a mouse, but I told her about my boots and showed her my feet. My toes were red raw.

'Jesus!' she exclaimed. 'What can we do to help them warm up?'

There really wasn't much I could do other than just take the pain until my feet thawed out inside the sleeping bag! It was fucking brutal, and made harder still by the fact that I knew it was all going to happen again the next day, and the day after that! As soon as I'd wake in the morning, I'd have to put on my frozen-solid wetsuit boots and go through it all again. As it turned out, I would walk the entire east coast of Scotland and into England wearing wetsuit boots! I wouldn't wish it on my worst enemy! With the weight of the bag on my back and my body weight, I can promise you, they offered zero cushioning, and standing on any stone was painful as hell, and equally frustrating. At times, I even remember thinking to myself: *I'd rather have to put up with the summer midges than this* – and that's saying something.

After four days of filming, Tim and Tom set off back to Swansea, to edit and await our next instalment of filming as we headed further down the coast in around a month's time. Apart from the feet situation, the whole experience was great. All of us had had a wonderful time and new friendships had blossomed. We each had a great work ethic and worked from early morning until late at night to make sure we did this documentary justice, not knowing at this point that the film would go on to win both a BAFTA and a Royal Television Award.

About a month before lockdown was over, we found a small lump by the side of one of Jet's nipples. Needless to say, the worry set in and I couldn't help but think the unthinkable. I remember very well saying to Kate, 'It's okay, we'll get it sorted,' putting on a brave face. I told her I needed to make a trip to the shop, as holding in how I really felt had just become too much. As soon as Jet and I were out of sight of Kate, I broke down in tears. As Jet sniffed around the trees exploring the smells of the forest, all the what-ifs flooded my mind. I did my very best not to let Jet see how much my recent discovery had upset me, so as not to make her anxious, knowing how well dogs can intuitively pick up on how we feel.

While we were in our lockdown camp, the locals had been incredible, always offering us help if needed. One lady in particular, Sarah Fowleigh, couldn't do enough to help. Aside from dropping off bags of coal by the nearby road where I would then use a blue trolley to drag one bag at a time down to camp, when she heard about Jet, she messaged us to say that she had booked an appointment at the vet for her and would cover the cost. The kindness of strangers came up trumps once again and, delighted as I was, as we simply didn't have the funds, it made me feel incredibly irresponsible and helpless. As it turned out, we had spotted the cancerous growth so early that only a small operation was needed and Jet was safe. But, given my affection for Jet, I was still worried sick and couldn't help fearing the worst. I found it hard seeing her taken into the vets on a lead while I stood and waited outside (the rules at the time due to Covid). We'd never left each other's side, and as she was guided in, she turned her head towards me helplessly, looking and wondering why the hell I was letting a stranger take her away. It broke my heart!

All of the other people who had their dogs in the vets were sat in their cars on their phones chatting away. I felt a little sad that for one or two, it seemed that their dog being here was a massive inconvenience. I kept telling myself, *That's the difference between dog owners and dog lovers!*

About an hour after Jet had left my side, I could clearly hear her high-pitched bark. I knew Jet had huge anxiety issues not being with me, so, to reassure her, I jumped up to the window and repeatedly shouted, 'It's okay, Jet! I'm here, girl! Don't worry, I'm here!' Before I knew it, the vet came outside and gave me a telling-off! 'Chris, there are other dogs in here under anaesthetic. Please can you keep the noise down!'

At the time I felt like telling her to fuck off – that's my dog and if I want to let her know I'm here, I will!

Looking back, I was clearly being overprotective, but to me she wasn't just a dog; she was my safe place, my constant source of happiness. When she wasn't by my side, I felt uneasy, and I knew that she felt the same. Kate managed to drag me away so as not to piss off the vet and sat me down on a park bench trying to console me until I received the call that Jet was ready to come out. When I saw her, I ran up and cuddled her like I would have my own children!

'Let's get away from here, mate, and take you back to our camp where you belong with your mum and dad,' I said, thanking the vet. Jet licked my face out of pure joy from having us back together and I breathed a huge sigh of relief knowing the lump had been removed.

During the second lockdown, Kate and I loved posting on social media about how many good people were out there in times where media news and papers talked of nothing but Covid. From elderly ladies scrambling through the woods to bring us a freshly made cake, to lovely locals and followers phoning up nearby shops to leave a couple of quid behind the till so we could pick up supplies, or just a quick social distancing visit to ask if we were all okay, to bags of coal left on the road for me to pick up and keep us warm at night, the human kindness we'd received had blown us away.

For the whole duration of lockdown, Kate and I had worked incredibly hard to keep ourselves entertained, healthy and fit. With the amount of intense time Kate and I were spending together, it was apparent that what we had was working. We were a great team. Kate's thirst to learn about living in the great outdoors – in a brutally cold winter, I might add – was unstoppable and she did so without a single moan. We had also become creative and together started discussing adventures that we could do once we'd finished the walk. Not once did one of us say anything that we both didn't agree on.

In early March 2021, after two months of living in a lockdown home, Nicola Sturgeon finally gave the all clear for Scotland to start making their way back out on the streets once again. It had been longer than the first lockdown; however, this second one had been a whole different experience for me, having had somebody else to share it with as opposed to being completely alone on the uninhabited island of Hildasay.

Kate and I were still in the early stages of our relationship – the honeymoon period if you like – but there was no doubt that a chance meeting at the Whaligoe Steps was blossoming into something wonderful. My dog loved her and now the people that had followed my journey from the beginning were starting to fall in love with her too. If truth be told, it really isn't hard! My life and my future were starting to take shape by this point, and even now, as I sit here writing, I often think back to just before starting the walk and remind myself of the importance of taking massive chances and following your heart. I still can't imagine where I would be now had I not decided just to get up and start walking. I would not have met Kate, and I would not have Jet by my side – that much I do know.

We were so glad to have kept ourselves away from

sitting in front of a television that pumped out sadness, and made a point of focusing on tales of kindness and giving out positive vibes ourselves! We thought, if we can be camped up on the northeast coast of Scotland during winter, with very little money and just a little battery power to stay connected with loved ones, and remain positive throughout, then we hoped that it would inspire others to do the same. Deep down, we felt like we'd achieved something, and it felt good. Thank you so much to all of the people who, in any way, shape or form, helped us to survive through lockdown two.

By the end of March, the snow and the cold had started to subside, and the woodland had started to blossom with snowdrops, daffodils and various other spring plants and flowers showing us the signs that winter was behind us and the warmer sun would soon be on its way. Spring is such a wonderful time of year, especially when you're living outside. I can recall every single year I've been on this walk the moment I first felt genuine warmth on my skin from the sun. It's always been a tradition for me that on the first day that this happened, I would stop for the day and soak up some vitamin D and allow the warmth of the sun to wrap around me as you would a warm blanket in the height of winter. It was such a wonderful feeling – almost a rebirth if you like. I felt myself taking more deep, long sighs of sheer relief, safe in the know-ledge that winter was finally over, and better weather was on the horizon. Every winter on this walk had been brutal in its own way, and this one was no exception. Never were we able to just walk into a home and put the heating on. Through autumn and winter, we simply had to accept that the next time we would feel warmth would be when nature decided to give it to us, and that could be a long wait! But, boy, when it does, it makes it all feel more than worth it.

By early April, we had preparations underway for leaving camp and getting ready to resume the walk. We were excited to get going again, yet slightly sad given the effort we'd put in to make our wooden lockdown home. While we were busy disassembling what we had built, we noticed that both mine and Kate's hair had gotten to a point where we were beginning to look like Bob Marley wannabes. Armed with a rusty pair of scissors, we headed down to the shoreline to give each other a makeshift haircut only days before we were due to leave. Given how much of a wind-up merchant I am – a character trait Kate is well aware of – I was shocked that she would trust me to cut her hair; it was just my sense of humour to do some over-enthusiastic hedge-hacking! But she simply sat down on a rock by the sea and I got to work snipping away at what was now a great example of a cavewoman's hair. After I finished, I admired my work. 'You look like a Toni and Guy model, if I do say so myself!' I chuckled.

She then asked for the scissors to return the favour, and I told her where to stick it! Given the fact that we share the same personalities, I knew I'd come away looking like an electric shock victim. Thanks, but no thanks, babe.

We stripped down most of our lockdown home to leave it as we found it, although we decided to leave the two side walls and back walls up, as we thought it would be fun for local families with their children to come and explore once we had left. The walls were perfectly safe and incredibly well built, and to this day, three years later, we still get the odd message with a photo showing us the still-standing walls with children messing around inside. It makes us smile each time. With camp now packed up, our kit sorted and bursting at the seams with excitement, we returned to Slains Castle where we'd left off to get back on the walk.

Slains Castle was the inspiration for Count Dracula's castle, and camping up in the grounds overlooking the sea crashing over the rocks at night was a truly atmospheric experience. From here, we racked up the miles heading onwards through the quaint villages of Cruden Bay, Whinnyfold and Collieston. The landscape was a lovely mix of spiky cliffs with outlets of rocks, golden beaches, a simple coast path and the occasional sea stack.

Despite it being April and us hoping that winter was firmly behind us, another cold spell hit and we found ourselves resuming the walk with another blast of snow upon us. The snow continued as we cracked on along the vast sandy beach of Newburgh, camping out amid its towering sand dunes and the granite city, Aberdeen, once again. By the time we walked through our lockdown woods, spring seemed to have firmly set in for good and we thoroughly enjoyed soaking up some much-needed days of sun as we pushed on through the picturesque bay of St Cyrus and into Arbroath, famous for its kippers.

Despite having set off walking again, which felt great and gave us a whole new focus each day, I still couldn't shake the one thing that was niggling at me all the time: the change in laws when it came to wild camping as we crossed over into England. It's one thing to be on your own and, like so many times I'd done before, sneak around or, as I like to call it, 'keep low, move fast' and get away with wild camping relatively unscathed, but I now had a dog and, of course, Kate with me too.

By this point we were mainly surrounded by small towns, villages and the occasional city, and far more agricultural land than what Jet and I had been used to on the west coast or the islands, and one of our biggest problems was sourcing water. We were now unable to drink from freshwater burns (streams), knowing the kind of stuff that gets washed into them from farmlands, which meant we would be carrying all our water. Soon enough summer would hit, meaning huge amounts were required for the three of us. This really got to me, given how much I loved the purity of the water I'd been drinking fresh from mountain burns over the past three years, plus the fact that I hadn't needed to carry it. The thought of tap water felt so dirty and, to be honest, so did bottled water, which was so artificial compared to what I'd been used to. Once we crossed the border, it was going to be a lot of sneaking around to find spots that were out of sight and out of mind of others, all with an extra 10 kilos of weight added to our bags with the water.

There would also be sections of coastline that we would not be able to walk due to private landowners, power stations and parts that had been cordoned off as wildlife sanctuaries. Industrial works alongside endless villages, towns and cities meant that the whole dynamic of the walk would soon be changing. Sooner or later, I had to accept that pretty much everything I loved about the walk would be gone: the freedom, the ability to drink clean water from mountain burns, bathing in those burns, the clean seas and, of course, the all-important fire-making! If I'm honest, before I'd even left, I was already looking forward to getting back to Scotland.

However, we were not gone yet, and still had two big estuaries to conquer that would take us from Dundee to Perth and then on to Stirling. It would then be onward to Edinburgh, leaving only 50-odd miles until the border. I was determined to make the most of this and kept my reservations about crossing the border to myself so as not to ruin it for Kate. Bless the poor woman, she'd joined this walk to seek adventure, and soon enough, everything I'd told her that had got her so excited over the phone before joining me would be gone! I continuously assured myself we would find a way to keep the adventure alive as we headed further south. I had an inkling that I was going to find the sudden changes challenging, but in retrospect I had no idea quite how difficult it would get.

11

Trouble in Dundee

It would be about two weeks before we hit our next coastal city, Dundee, which starts on the Firth of Tay estuary. Once again, Kate and I talked about sleeping rough in the city centre to highlight homelessness, just like we did in Aberdeen. I mean this with no disrespect to Dundee, but given the fact that it was May bank holiday weekend and the first weekend of the lifted lockdown to boot, I knew that the pissed-up masses would be pouring out onto the streets of Dundee ready to let loose! Having just been kept inside for months, in my eyes, sleeping rough under such circumstances would be a recipe for disaster – or at least there would be a serious chance of an unwanted encounter!

After a rather heated debate, knowing how much Kate wanted us to be a 50:50 team and have an equal role in everything we did, I managed to get my way and persuade her to stay just on the outskirts and allow me to go in alone with Jet. I couldn't live with myself if anything were to happen to her, so I point blank refused to have such a burden on my shoulders. She was genuinely annoyed with me, but I hope she had some understanding that it was only because I loved and cared for her. I left Kate and headed into Dundee city centre to spend the night sleeping rough alone. It wouldn't be long before my point to Kate was proved, and for the first time in years, hostility would be thrown my way.

It was the weekend, and the city of Dundee was heaving with alcohol-fuelled youngsters enjoying their newfound freedom after four months of remaining housebound. I knew I could handle myself, so I wasn't majorly worried; if anything, I just couldn't be arsed with any trouble. My days of being tanked up in a city, ready for any mischief, were long gone. The older I get, the more I stay away from any kind of confrontation. Life is simply too short! When you're young you often feel invincible, especially if you've been in the Paras as I have. But with age that feeling subsides and you start to develop a sense of self-preservation. Colds last longer, the flu hurts more, and bones take longer to heal. Even a hangover goes from what was once a funny call to your mate laughing about how rotten you feel to now an epically big deal where you feel you should be tucked away in a hospital on an intravenous drip of painkillers! Basically, I've got a lot more sensible with age.

I knew that slowly but surely the evening streets would start to empty in the next few hours, and I looked around for a place to lay down the sleeping bag for the night. I started a video to post on my social media, keeping my followers updated, letting them know what I was up to and where I was. It was a busy but peaceful atmosphere, with people singing and enjoying their newfound freedom. Jet was on a lead, and I noticed she was gaining distance from me as the cord unravelled from the plastic casing in my left hand. I turned my head towards her and, as I did so, I suddenly heard an almighty yelp from my girl and saw a fella with his leg still half extended. Jet fell to the floor and, just like that and for the first time in as long as I can remember, I saw red.

With my bag still on my shoulders, I dropped the lead and my phone and ran at the guy. In my eyes, he may as well have just kicked a newborn baby. Without even a second thought, and the weight of my body and bag behind me, I grabbed him hard and pinned him against a wall, making sure he immediately regretted his decision. With my hand around his jawbone, I turned to my left to see Jet standing, but clearly in discomfort. Very quickly, I regained control of my thoughts as a group of his friends grappled with my wrists and backpack to get me off and loosen the clamp that I had around him. Now conscious and less misty-eyed, I could hear his friend saying, 'I am so sorry! I'd be fucking mad if I was you and it was my dog. He's a twat and we will make sure he knows it and will regret this tomorrow!' I let go, ran over to Jet and hugged her so tight, checking for any injuries. Fortunately, she was not kicked on the same side as her relatively fresh wound from her operation.

I saw a couple of his friends drag the attacker off to the taxi rank and throw him inside a cab. They came back to me and could not have been more apologetic while giving Jet hugs and cuddles. I just walked away. With age, I can say my days of being among drunken people are well behind me; I'll take a fire in a mountain pub over a city pub full of drunks any day of the week. It was the first time on my walk so far that I felt that I was slowly returning to all the things that I'd originally wanted to get away from. But Jet was okay; that was the main thing. As we made our way back towards Kate and away from the city centre, I really believe I left a little piece of me in Dundee that evening, a slice of my happiness shattered for ever. Whether it was the reminder that I was coming back into the real world, or perhaps the idea that for the first time since Jet and I first crossed paths, I'd let her down, I wasn't sure, but one thing I did know – as we walked away, I promised myself I would never ever let that happen again.

A few hours later, Jet and I returned to Kate. She could obviously tell something was up and while I sat nurturing Jet, Kate noticed that the knuckles on my right hand were bleeding. I was so embarrassed. Believe me when I say I am the least aggressive man that you will ever meet, and it would kill me if Kate thought that I was some kind of scrapper.

She was not exactly over the moon, but knowing how much I love Jet, and of course, how much she loved her, she completely understood once I told her what had happened. She gave us both the biggest, warmest hug, and we both decided from this point on that for Jet's sake and for our own safety, we would now avoid sleeping rough on the streets. Instead, we would visit homeless shelters, talk to homeless people, and do whatever else we could along the way.

From Dundee, we headed around the estuary to Perth and then back up the other side that would take us to St Andrews. The estuary was around 15 miles one way and about 30 miles back up the other side, and the walk around it was very flat, with some woodland flanked by ongoing reedbeds and lots of open agricultural land to navigate. I had my forty-first birthday as we were walking back up towards St Andrews. It was 6 May and we pitched our tent for the night in some woods along the estuary bank and once again found ourselves near penniless, eating whatever our little change could purchase from a local shop.

It turned out, however, that a lovely couple by the name of Janet and Bill got in touch to say they wanted to find us in the woodlands and bring us either a curry or a Chinese takeaway, and spend a birthday dinner with us. Kate was delighted, as I knew that she felt a bit guilty that we were unable to do anything special to celebrate. I felt I already had everything I needed, but the sound of a takeaway did tickle my fancy, I must admit, and the offer was very kind. That night around the fire, with decorations hanging overhead in the trees, myself, Kate, Jet, Bill and Janet sat and devoured an Indian takeaway and a bottle of wine. While tucking in, I thought back to my last birthday, which had been on Hildasay. Never in a million years would I have thought that I'd be spending my next birthday still so far up north because of the lockdown – and having gained an extra member of the team with an amazing girlfriend who would walk alongside me. I silently chuckled at how much I loved the uncertainty of adventure. It has its ups, and it has its downs, but the amazing times far outweigh the hardships.

Four days after my birthday, we finally arrived in St Andrews, the town where William and Kate got together, and *my* Kate was determined to give me the grand tour of this incredibly posh town where she'd spent years studying Spanish and French at its prestigious university. She was excited to show me where she once lived, and we visited the beautiful cathedral ruins and some of Kate's old digs, where she was kind enough to recite some of the antics she got up to. But, as with any other town, I was eager just to make it through to the other side and move on. In my experience of walking, the more affluent the place, the less people were interested in what we were doing and few, if any, donations to the charity would come in. St Andrews was no different as it turned out.

There were some lovely moments, nonetheless. After a hard day's graft along the coast, we reached the Keys pub, where we met a local sand artist who made a fantastic piece of art for us down on Castle Sands the next day. We may have left the town in bucketing rain, but his kindness left me beaming! After a few days touring around all of St Andrews, now feeling like that husband who has been dragged around the shops on his wife's birthday, it was time to move on to Stirling.

Inside me, there was a deep sense of excitement. So many times throughout my walk while looking at the maps, my eyes would wander over to the right-hand side of the UK map and land at Edinburgh, knowing that once I was there, Scotland would be in the bag, with only around 50 miles until I hit the border at Berwick upon Tweed. I knew reaching Edinburgh would be a monumental if bittersweet moment for me personally.

We made our way down the Firth of Forth estuary towards Stirling, all the while knowing that Edinburgh was on the other side of the estuary, which we couldn't see due to the fog. We pitched up for a couple of days to rest on the lovely beach just outside Elie and Earlsferry. It had been pretty overcast and misty when we arrived and first set up camp, so visibility was very poor, but as the evening drew in, the clouds and mist lifted and as we sat finishing the stew we'd cooked over the fire, for the first time I could see Edinburgh with my own eyes! I'm not sure why I didn't share this moment with Kate or Jet, but I felt a surge of pure elation, pride and self-achievement in every cell in my body.

Without saying a thing, I stood up and started walking towards the sea, now a few hundred yards away due to the outgoing tide. The walk turned into a jog and as tears of joy started streaming down my face, my running pace turned into a sprint. Wearing all my clothes, I barged into the water to waist height, shouting at the top of my voice: 'I told you! I told you! I fucking told you I'd get to Edinburgh!'

I turned in the direction of Kate and Jet and shouted, 'We did it, Jet! We bloody did it!' Kate, aware that she was witnessing a monumental personal moment and knowing how much this meant to me, also had tears running down her cheeks. My two girls ran down to me in the surf, Jet stopping at the water's edge while Kate plunged in fully dressed to give me a cuddle. Happily soaked to the bone, we sat with Jet and stared at our final Scottish city. There is no real way to describe a feeling like this, but in hindsight, what it was really about was the fact that I hadn't quit! Only I knew how testing and tough it had been to get to this point. For the rest of my life, I'll be able to revisit in my mind snapshots of this journey and take myself back there whenever I choose with a simple closing of my eyelids. Memories are and will always be far more powerful than any photo or description, because they belong to you and you alone. In the crazy, fast-paced, social media-dominated, phone-camera-obsessed, click-of-a-button world we live in today, I feel that is truly something to treasure.

We made our way along the estuary towards Stirling where, just outside of a town called Kirkcaldy, a wonderful couple offered us the use of their man shed. David came to the coast to pick us up and take us back to his house, and it was immediately evident that he was a real character. My word, he loved to talk, and if you weren't familiar with a thick Scottish accent, he may as well have been speaking another language! Kate and I really took to him and his wife, Caroline. There was something about them that embodied the things that I loved so much about Scotland – outgoing, friendly, talkative, and incredibly welcoming people with an 'our home is your home' kind of attitude.

'If you want food or a drink, you know where the kitchen is – I'm not getting it for you, you lazy shit!' said David. Yet every night, evening meals were delivered to the shed with either whisky or beer to accompany the meal. David would sit and tell us stories over dinner and after only a few days and nights, we knew we had made some new friends. On the last evening, David brought out Superman and Superwoman onesie pyjamas for Kate and me to wear as a refreshing change from the clothes we wore daily. We loved the humour of it and couldn't help doing our best Superman impressions in costume!

That night, Caroline joined us in the shed with David and we sunk a few beers as he gave me his guitar (which he had no idea how to play) to get some Scottish tunes going. We sang some great songs, including 'Caledonia', and discovered Caroline had the most beautiful voice. Sadly, and I know David will find this funny, his passion for a good old singalong with four or five Tennent's in his belly meant his horrendous voice overshadowed Caroline's and completely ruined her dulcet tones! As I played guitar, I looked at Kate trying my very best not to burst out laughing. He thought he was magnificent, and despite the monstrosity of his performance, I had to hand it to him – his ability to get lost in the moment was more powerful than anything else going on in the room!

Without us knowing, this would be the last time we'd participate in Scottish cultural live music in a tiny garden shed accompanied by awful singing and an abundance of Tennent's lager, while dressed in Superman nightwear! We still had about 80 miles to Kirkcaldy, where we were to stay before we finished Scotland. The night was an intimate little send-off before we hit England in around a week's time, and we loved it. To make it even more special, as we said our goodbyes, Caroline presented us with a beautiful pendant that she had made with our names engraved upon it.

Soon enough, we hit Stirling, which I found exciting, as during my walk in Scotland I had become very interested in the Scottish clans and the Wallace and Robert the Bruce movement. The William Wallace story I believe resonated with a lot of people because of his fight for freedom rather than power. To me personally the famous battle of Stirling where Wallace defeated the English was not just a win for Scotland, but more so a win for the common person. We visited the site of the impressive castle (though we couldn't afford to go in) and of course the famous Wallace Monument.

Before we knew it, we would find ourselves taking the first steps into Edinburgh, where we would once again meet Tim and Tom for another four days of filming in and around the capital. Now that it was spring and winter was firmly behind us, it made the whole filming experience a lot easier and a real pleasure to be part of. Kate and I were both so pleased that, as well as filming, we were able to link up with several local people from the homeless charity Shelter, to talk to them about their experiences and share them on our social media.

With the company of the production crew, we felt safe enough to sleep rough that night on the streets of Edinburgh, but it would be our last time. Before night set in, we put out a post saying we were in the city centre if anyone wanted to come and say hello. We were absolutely blown away by the number of people who showed up after work to chat to us, lend their support and even bring us gifts – another testament to that wonderful Scottish hospitality – and we were so happy that examples of the kindness we'd received had been captured and broadcast nationwide. We believed that we were filming something very special, and hoped that the effort we'd put in would be reflected in the documentary itself.

The BBC had agreed to pay me £3,000 for our efforts, and it couldn't have come at a better time! A lot of our gear was in desperate need of replacing and, finally, I would be able to do what any normal walker had the privilege of doing: wear a pair of walking boots! Those thick wetsuit booties that I'd been suffering in for so long had taken their toll on my feet. After replacing our kit, we kept what small change we had for supplies and continued along the eastern coastline towards North Berwick, Dunbar, Eyemouth and the border of Scotland.

It was on this final stretch of Scottish coastline that I began to notice that my dear Jet was slowing down. There was just something about her that was telling me she was getting tired of this endless trek! To be fair, all those miles and challenging terrains she'd covered on the west coast and the islands were a lot to ask of any dog, plus the fact that she was getting older and was a little less energetic now. It started to play on my mind. Knowing summer was not far around the corner and we were heading further south, I would keep a close eye on her to make sure that I wasn't overexerting her in any way, shape or form. If Jet gave me the nod that we needed to stop, that's exactly what I would do. The loyalty and dedication Jet had shown me from day one reserved her right to be the only reason that I would ever stop this walk. I already had a plan mapped out in my head that, if need be, I'd build a buggy that she could sit in and I would tow her!

It was relatively flat and a really beautiful stretch of coast, with some lovely beaches, and along the way we would find lovely sections of forestry that made for perfect pitch-ups and an idyllic end to Scotland. In these last few days, I made the most of lighting fires for our evening meals and morning coffee. Once we crossed over into England, we would rarely be able to light our own fires due to the strict regulations, and so I tried to preserve a gas canister for what was to come. The dread of being back in England was ever-present.

Just before crossing the border, we stayed in a beautiful little village called St Abbs. The coastline here was stunning, with incredible rock formations and beautiful bays to feast our eyes on. We sat back here and took in the near completion of another country, first Northern Ireland and now Scotland. Actually, it was only me that had completed all of Scotland. I hadn't met Jet until I reached Ayrshire, and Kate didn't join the walk until Inverness!

On our very last night, we were blessed to meet a wonderful couple, Duncan and Joan, who offered us their caravan on a caravan site before we crossed the border. It was a very special little place and we went into town to get supplies for our last meal in Scotland, given that we actually had a working oven at our disposal, and cooked ourselves a little roast dinner as a celebration. For some reason, I guess because I wanted to reflect on the enormity of the walk, I had an urge to be on my own for just an hour. Kate was incredibly understanding and emotionally intelligent; she knew that I wanted to say my own personal goodbye to a country that had helped me to change, heal and reshape my life. I walked to the shop with Jet and bought a small bottle of Famous Grouse, then went and sat in some woods.

As I nestled Jet between my legs and swigged on the whisky, I thought about some of the highlights of our time here – and, of course, some of the not-so-good times. But, as always, it's the most challenging times that you look back on with pride. I'd walked into Scotland lost and broken, but now I would leave her with a strong sense of purpose and as a more fulfilled and complete human than I'd ever been in my life. I knew what I wanted to do with the rest of my life, or at least what I didn't want, and that was to get dragged into the rat race and life of mundane routine. I wasn't exactly sure what I was going to be, but from here on I knew that I would pursue a life of adventure. For me it was all about following the heart, not the herd. I could achieve anything I set my mind to; the walk had proven that.

In Scotland, I had beaten depression and anxiety, rekindled my relationship with my daughter – my inspiration for setting off in the first place – and I knew that if there was ever a place where one day I were to settle, it would be up here; around like-minded people and a more relaxed, less hectic environment to live, where people took time to talk and helped each other in real, tightly knit communities. I had no intention of ever going back to a life of feeling like a cog in a corporate machine that would wear me down bit by bit until eventually it broke me. And, of course, the icing on the cake: my darling Jet and beautiful Kate had come into my life, fitting into my future plans like a hand in glove! I knew that my future was still uncertain, but it was bright. That dim flame relit on Llangennith beach, after a giant wave spat me onto the sand, had grown into a healthy, thriving fire, ready to take on anything. I was now a very happy man.

After an hour of pure reflection, I stood up and wiped away the twigs and leaves attached to my kilt from sitting on the woodland floor. My eyes salted with thick tears, then I took a deep breath and muttered quietly, 'Goodbye, Scotland, thank you for everything! England, let's 'ave ya.'

On the morning of the border crossing, our very last stretch was a coast path that ran along 100-foot sea cliffs with the omnipresent gulls gawking away as if they were celebrating this epic milestone with us. Our fundraising total was now sitting at £191,000, and Kate and I were determined to get it up to £200,000. This is where the power of social media can work wonders! As we made our way towards the border of England and Scotland, we put out a post on social media via a live feed so our followers could share this moment with us. To our disbelief, a large group of people came to welcome us into England and share in our goodbye to Scotland, including a bagpiper called Jamie who, adorned in full traditional attire, played us over the border. Others had travelled from as far as Newcastle and different areas of Scotland to say their farewells and hellos; it was so wonderful to experience such love and support on such a special, heartfelt occasion.

Astonishingly, as we ran a live feed, only a hundred yards from the 'Welcome to England' sign on the coast path, our fundraising leapt over the £200,000 mark – all within the space of around ten minutes! What a satisfying feeling, I can tell you! We spoke into the camera to say thank you to all of those that had in any way helped us along the Welsh, west of England, Northern Ireland and Scottish coast and islands on my UK walk. Kate and I held hands and, with Jet in between us, I took my first steps onto English soil in three and a half years. What a moment it was! I had first entered Scotland at the beginning of December 2017, and was leaving at the end of June 2021. Yes, two lockdowns had held me up, but it was my insistence on sticking so rigidly to the sections of wild and unpaved coastline that meant it had taken so long, and it was easily the hardest and most fulfilling experience of my life up to that point.

Once we'd said our goodbyes to all the lovely people that came to see us off from Scotland and welcome us into England, we found ourselves once again alone and ready to take on our next challenge. I couldn't help but be struck by the difference between the Scottish section of the border gate compared with the English side. The Scottish side had a rickety fence shielding anyone from taking a step too close to the cliff edge and into the sea, with grass kept short by the surrounding sheep and a wild feel about it. On the English side, in contrast, was a narrow strip of grass cut to perfection with a much grander fence that would lead us straight into a caravan park. I chuckled and thought this pretty summed up the difference between England and Scotland, at least the land ownership side of things!

'Buckle up, Kate!' I said. 'This is going to be interesting!'

PART TWO

Crossing Over

12

Hello, England!

It was late June 2021 and we'd started firmly getting our feet into England. It would still be a little while yet until we got to Newcastle, which gave us some all-important breathing space to process the thought that we would need to be a lot more particular about where we would set up camp. We had some wonderful places to hit before we reached Newcastle, including Lindisfarne (Holy Island), then Bamburgh and Alnmouth.

We were super excited to hit Holy Island, mostly because of its Viking history. I'd seen so many remnants of the Vikings in Northern Scotland that this period had become a real fascination for me. When it came to jaw-dropping landscapes, I knew full well I'd already seen the best coastlines the UK had to offer, but history is everywhere, which made anywhere interesting. We planned to soak it all up like a sponge, finding out what we could about the places we'd walk through to enjoy them all the more. Holy Island is connected to the mainland by a causeway, but as long as the tides are far enough out, you can walk over in a rather special fashion. We did the traditional pilgrim walk, taking our shoes off and sinking deep into the muddy marsh with each step over to the island.

The weather was glorious, and we were determined to make the most of our day, which was made all the easier when English Heritage invited us to come and explore the castle grounds, which were perfectly placed to give a bird's-eye view of any land or sea invasion. From the castle you could see the old cathedral, which was the first written-about place to be attacked by the Vikings, who savagely killed unarmed monks and took their treasures. The island was beautiful to walk around and we researched as much history as we could to share on our social media pages.

We felt so privileged and grateful. Kate, always the optimist, turned to me and said, 'This is special! You never know – if this is a sign of things to come, then England might prove more accommodating than we thought!' Maybe I'd be pleasantly surprised, but it would take a lot more than that to shake my scepticism.

We had brought all of our gear along with us in the hope of staying overnight on the island. However, that night we got our first taste of what was to become all too normal, when we were unequivocally told by locals that we were not allowed to camp on Holy Island. That's all well and good if you can jump in the car and head over the causeway road back to the mainland and find a nice camp spot, but this wasn't the case for us. Returning to the mainland to sleep would mean having to wait for the tide to allow us to wade back over, find a place to get supplies and stock up with water, and then find somewhere to sleep. It was already a world away from Scotland, and I can't begin to tell you how much this made me angry, unlike Kate, who always tried to make the best of a situation. Given that I had experienced such freedom over the past years, I knew these English rules would grind me down. To me, the right to camp is something that, within certain restrictions, we should all be entitled to. I had a constant thought in my mind: *Why is it okay to see hundreds of homeless people sleeping in bus stops, doorways and tents in the middle of the streets all around English cities, and yet two people and a dog trying to raise money for charity are constantly moved on?* It just didn't make sense to me, but it was something we were going to have to learn to live with over the next year. Fortunately, the reach of social media managed to get us a spot in someone's back garden that first night back in England.

I was absolutely delighted to hear that on the same day that we would reach Bamburgh, my lockdown family, Victor Lawrenson and his wife, Pauline, would be there too on holiday with Victor's parents. I was blown away by Bamburgh; wherever you went in this small village, you would have a different perspective of the most beautiful castle, which sat high above the settlement overlooking the sea. It was a truly stunning little place, and it was the first time that I had seen Victor, Pauline and Victor's mum and dad since leaving Hildasay. It was also the first time that Kate would get to meet these people I had spoken so much to her about. It was so good to see them as we sat down at a table outside a cafe and shared lunch together (it was on them, of course!). After a few hours with what I like to call my 'lockdown family', Kate, Jet and I headed off to find a place to pitch up for the night – only to find a message via my Facebook page from Bamburgh Castle!

Over the years, the castle had been upgraded from its early fifth-century days as a fort and has been owned by one family for generations. Having heard we had reached the area, the son of the owner had got in touch to offer us either a stable at his house or, if we wanted, a spot in the castle grounds. It was a no-brainer: castle grounds all the way! When we arrived at the castle we were shown where we were allowed to camp – a huge patch of grass that sat near the centre of the castle, overlooking all of Bamburgh on one side, and the beautiful coast on the other. We felt so privileged and, better still, it just so happened that when we turned up, a gentleman called Jamie was also staying there with two giant shire horses. Jamie was on his own mission, riding in a carriage with his two horses, Millie and Willem, travelling from his home in Herefordshire up into Scotland, a journey of around three months in total, to raise money for the police force his brother had served in before he died in a tragic car accident. Jamie had a clear love and passion for horses. With his broad-rim hat and leather jacket, he reminded me of an Indiana Jones type. We swapped stories of our adventures with a few beers, courtesy of Jamie. He was a larger-than-life character; a no-nonsense, no-bullshit bloke who, a very long time ago, had, like me, given up all of the madness and made a pact with himself not to surround himself with anybody who wasn't to his taste! He was a man completely comfortable in his own skin who was simply happy to spend his time around his horses. After one night at Bamburgh Castle together, I'm sure that Kate and I will remain lifelong friends with Jamie.

After a really special night spent in the grounds of Bamburgh Castle, it was time to get going again and power on further south. As we progressed through Newcastle, Sunderland, Seaham, Peterlee, Hartlepool and down to Middlesbrough, I would find myself in the most built-up areas I'd seen since leaving Liverpool just under four years ago. The succession of concrete and the absence of nature were a nightmare for camping, so, as we edged down the coast here, we had to start taking offers of garages, sheds and back gardens as places of refuge. We accepted that this was all part of the adventure and, on the positive side, we looked forward to the opportunity of meeting new people and spending some time with them. The walk was all about balance: as our popularity grew with endless radio interviews and local newspaper articles, people would look for us as we walked through their areas. They wanted to welcome us, shake our hands and, obviously, those interactions would come with an array of questions. Ninety per cent of the time these were always the same, which could get tedious, but I would remind myself that although it was my millionth time replying, it was a first for them.

Being a bit of a loner and enjoying my own space, the place we chose to pitch up camp and settle in for the night would be our opportunity to switch off, prepare for the next day, and have some much-needed rest from walking, or even thinking about the walk, if only for a couple of hours. What would soon become apparent is that when lovely people offered us somewhere to sleep for the night, quite understandably, we would often spend the evening being asked questions until we were well and truly worn out and just needing to go to bed ready to do it all again tomorrow. Having said this, at this point it was all still relatively new to us, so it really wasn't much of a problem at all. But even so, when we were in built-up areas – and I mean this with no disrespect – I was always eager to get out the other side!

When we eventually hit Middlesbrough, my worst nightmare had come true: to get through the city, we would have to walk across a large industrial area that was situated on a huge estuary, of which both sides were incredibly built up, unlike in other industrial estates, where we could just pass through without having to cross over water. We'd have to cross the bridge over the estuary that would take us through to the other side – around a two-day walk with Jet in the summer heat. Worse still, when we arrived, we found out that the main bridge had been closed off and we would have to walk our way around a huge industrial section in order to cross another bridge further down the estuary! With Jet's pace slowing and the fact that she detested loud noises, pavements, banging machinery and tiny paths with steel gates next to busy roads with beeping cars screaming past us, I was dreading the prospect. Jet also had to stay on the lead, which slowed her even more, and so it was looking like it would take us around four days to get back to the coastline, with absolutely no idea where on earth we would camp each night. It was a total disaster! Alone, I could've run the whole shebang in a day and got the hell out of there, but that wasn't possible now – I had my two girls, and where I went, they went. That's just how we rolled. Admittedly, I had a face like a slapped arse; what a shit four days this was going to be!

I've always been a firm believer that when least expected, life can often throw you a rainbow-coloured lifeline. And in this case, this is exactly what happened. It was a really warm day and we had stocked up with water and rations, at least as much as I could carry, mostly tins of dog food and dry food for Jet in the hope that, along the way, Kate and I would find somewhere that we could eat. One perk of being in busier areas was the abundance of cafes! I had a right grump on as we sat in a car park, preparing ourselves for the four-day trek around busy industrial areas, whilst Jet sniffed around a few yards away from me.

Kate got up and said she needed a wee, so headed to a public toilet a few hundred yards away. This was another problem that we would have as we walked through this section; there's nothing worse than needing the toilet and having absolutely nowhere to go. We knew this might happen, so any kind of relief while the opportunity was there was a given! When she left, I was just about to put my phone onto airplane mode to save battery when I took one last look and saw a message sent just a few minutes before:

> *Chris, I have been following your adventures for a while now and I hear that you are somewhere near Middlesbrough! My name is Dave, and I am currently sailing around the UK in my two-mast sailing boat, visiting lifeboat stations! As I type, I'm just about to go past the estuary that heads down into Middlesbrough! If you would like to come and see the boat or even if we can give you a lift over the estuary rather than walk it, I'll be more than happy to come and pick you up!*
>
> *The boat has a blue bottom and white masts; if you're on the coast near Middlesbrough, there's a good chance you may be able to spot us! Anyway, it would be great to hear from you, if not, good luck on your adventures!*

With that, I stood up and looked over to my left out to sea, and would you believe it – there it bloody was! It was like the final scene of *The Goonies* as the pirate ship sees light for the first time. My eyes couldn't believe what they were seeing. A surge of almost panic consumed my body at the thought that, somehow, I might miss this opportunity! My hands almost shaking, I replied immediately, trying my very best not to show my desperation. 'This would be incredible pal! What a lovely experience that would be. I couldn't be more grateful!' I wrote back.

I sent my number, and he phoned me straight away. What a turn of events – and especially when we really needed it. It was one of those rare and beautiful moments in life.

Kate returned from the toilet expecting a very deflated man, knowing that we were just about to set off on our four-day industrial walk.

'Kate, Kate!' I shouted. 'You're not going to bloody believe this! I've got us a ride over the estuary by boat!' She smiled, a confused look on her face, wondering if I was winding her up. 'I've arranged an RV (rendezvous) about a mile from here on a small beach where we'll get picked up, but we need to go now!'

Filled with enthusiasm, we picked up our bags and did our best to run to the pick-up point. The beautiful two-mast sailing boat had dropped anchor about half a mile down the estuary, its sails shimmering in the baking sun. Then I spotted a small rib heading in our direction to collect us. I gave Kate the biggest hug and dropped to my knees to give Jet one too.

'What are the bloody chances?' I marvelled.

Before we knew it, we were buzzing along on the rib to the boat that would have us across the estuary in twenty-five minutes. It was precarious lifting Jet from the rib and onto the boat, but we managed it and soon jumped aboard to meet Dave, a man who, with his salty blonde hair and all-around mariner's air, looked like he'd been at sea all his life. Aside of him there was a four-man crew. We settled in with a cup of coffee and were given a tour of the most beautiful wooden sailing boat that I had ever clapped eyes on. I love the fact that it was propelled by wind through its sails rather than being engine-driven. Kate and I were shown how it worked and even had the privilege of taking turns at being skipper of this beautiful vessel, our saviour of the day! It was just the kind of boat you'd imagine James Bond in at the end of the film with a beautiful girl on his arm. We soon arrived back on land and said our goodbyes. We couldn't thank Dave enough. I'm not sure he and his crew realized just how much we appreciated the lovely gesture, but the perfect timing was heaven sent! We really savoured the moment and walked a further few miles down the beach then camped up for the evening. How lovely to have a night to ourselves, knowing what we *could've* been doing at that moment. Perfect.

Having just passed through this run of built-up areas, we were now looking forward to our next stretch of coastline, which would take us through Redcar, Saltburn-by-the-Sea, Staithes and into Whitby. These would be less densely populated areas compared to what we had just been through. Having spent many nights in garages and sheds over this last section, we'd really missed the tent, so we made a pact between us to somehow find a way to wild camp for the whole of the Yorkshire coast. Kate had grown up in Yorkshire but had never seen this side of its coast, so was in excited spirits to walk it. Furthermore, once we hit Whitby, I would be meeting Kate's dad for the first time – something I was slightly nervous about.

Yorkshire gave us a great stretch of coastline with an excellent coastal path that ran pretty much all the way through down to Whitby. Wild camping was much easier, with plenty of places where we could keep out of sight in very picturesque spots with no worries of getting moved on. Along the way were some lovely quaint villages where we would stop for a pick-me-up coffee before moving on to find a camp spot for the evening. Weather-wise, we were now well and truly into the furnace of summer, and each day it seemed to be getting hotter. I love walking through the heat, as does Kate, but my little girl Jet was not so keen on the sunrays; for a while now we'd been having to wake up and get going at the crack of dawn just to get a few hours' walking in before the intense midday heat. At this point we would break and resume again later on in the cooler hours to avoid Jet burning up. This meant very early starts and long days, with it often being really late before we found our spot to pitch for the night. In addition, water supplies were more in demand now, as we drank greater quantities in the hotter weather. The extra weight of about 10–15 litres of water to drag to our camp spot on top of all the rest of our gear was quite frankly hideous!

The trickiest thing about wild camping along this Yorkshire stretch was that once we'd picked up our food and water supplies from a local shop in the nearest town or village, we would then inevitably have to trek a good few miles extra to find somewhere where we felt convinced that we wouldn't get moved on. With the food in our bergens, Kate laden with any surplus supplies that wouldn't fit in, and me carrying five litres of water in each hand, we walked until we found a spot and set up before dark. It was always a slog; slow, burdened with so much weight. By the time we'd reached a suitable camp spot, we were always absolutely shattered.

As soon as the camping spot was chosen, I would drop my bag and the bottle of water to the floor. I couldn't even process the fact I was going to have to do this for another couple of thousand miles! Some days I felt like that guy Sisyphus in Greek mythology, who pushes the boulder all the way up to the top of the hill, only to see it roll down again. I'd do my best to show Kate that carrying that huge bottle was no big deal. We needed water, I had to carry it and that was that. It was hard graft, but I took some comfort in knowing that over time I would get more used to it, and it would become easier.

We were now having to spend our time around more and more people once again. In our moments alone, Kate and I would make the most of time together and rather than talk about the walk, we'd discuss things like future adventures and even the prospect of one day starting a family together. The time we spent together was so intense that we both agreed that we knew each other as well in the space of under one year as most couples would living together for a decade. If we could live in each other's pockets as we had and still enjoy one another's company every day, then our connection had strong legs for a long-term future. She was the female version of myself and Jet adored her. She is such a grafter; fun, loving and a wonderful soul – one of those rare people that, no matter who she meets, leaves their lives that little bit brighter.

I remember watching her while we were on the sailing

boat heading over the estuary from Middlesbrough, chatting so confidently and articulately to the boat crew about their adventures and how their sailing voyage worked. I couldn't help but think how serendipitous it all felt – the chance of this boat being in exactly the same spot as we were was as slim as the chance it took for me to be down the bottom of the Whaligoe Steps at the same time as Kate! It was easy to remind myself that the best things in life really do come when you least expect them. But also, that if you are destined to be with somebody, the universe will do everything it can to place you in each other's path.

13

Whitby and the curious case of the red-purple legs

Soon enough and around 20 miles south down the coast, we arrived in Whitby. If Slains Castle was the inspiration for Dracula's homestead, then Whitby was the place where Bram Stoker sat down and wrote the story in his hotel room directly opposite the cemetery. And you can see all these inspirations in his legendary story; as the captain of the *Demeter* ship, dead and tied to the wheel, arrives in a storm, and a huge black wolf leaps up the cliff towards the old snaggled tombstones.

Now August, summer was in full swing, and the tourists were massing like flies around fruit. On arriving in the town, we had a short meeting with the local mayor, and it soon became apparent that because of the tourist season, certain sections of the coast, including Whitby, would be as busy as it could get. Picturesque as it is, with its warren of narrow streets filled with independent shops, the place was absolutely rammed! It was difficult even walking Jet without her getting trodden on by the maze of people on the high street. For me, it was the wrong time of year to be here, but at least we had our plans to meet up with Kate's father, Ian, and stepmother, Val.

I was excited to meet them for the first time and certainly appreciated the effort they had made to fly all the way from Abu Dhabi to see Kate, and for Ian to meet this homeless walker his daughter had fallen in love with! Obviously, like any man, I was keen to make a good impression. I was a 41-year-old guy and, although about as unconventional as they come, had plenty of life experience behind me. I hoped for Kate's sake that they would both warm to me. Ian is a man of few words and as I met him for the first time outside his B&B, like many dads, I could sense his protectiveness over his daughter and felt he was still somewhat sceptical about all that she had given up just to be with me. He did have a very dry sense of humour though, a trait that I really liked about him, and I hoped he was beginning to warm to me as I was to him.

That evening after dinner, and before Ian and Val retreated to their bed and breakfast, Kate and I needed to find somewhere to camp. It was already gone 10 p.m. and it wasn't the easiest task to find somewhere quickly in the dark, but from the backseat of the car we spotted a place that looked good enough and asked Ian to pull into a layby to drop us off. It was here that I witnessed a much softer side of Ian. Having done this for so long

The morning after Kate and I camped at the bottom of the Whaligoe Steps together. I even made her a coffee before I made one for myself – trust me, that is not something I would do for just anyone!

Kate and I busy making our lockdown shelter.

(*above*) At our firepit, ready to hang our cooking pot. We would make our own food every night during lockdown.

(*left*) Kate had come straight from the warmth of a home and London city life to a blisteringly cold winter on the northeast coast of Scotland. It must have been love!

(*above*) A moment of elation. I ran into the sea looking at Edinburgh, my last city in Scotland, a landmark showing I was nearing the end of my Scottish adventure.

(*right*) After four hours of surgery, Jet made it through her operation. Riddled with nerves and shaken by panic attacks, I'm quite sure I was more of a mess than she was. Vet Scott Miller will forever be on my Christmas card list!

The two-mast sailing vessel that saved us from having to walk many extra miles around the industrial coast of Middlesbrough when the bridge was broken. It's little moments like this that make you think someone's looking out for you.

Kate walked pregnant until only a few weeks before she gave birth to Magnus. Our colourful yurt by the coast was where we had planned for Kate to have a water birth. It didn't pan out that way, but that's life!

Had I not met Jet and changed the pace of my walk to accommodate her, I would never have met Kate and probably would have finished a year earlier. I still have to pinch myself. That one decision to do this walk brought me to all I now have.

The trusty VW T4 that we got once Magnus was born – thanks to our friend Steve Roorke. If I'm honest, the fact that Jet was ageing and less capable definitely swayed me to get this van, probably more so than having Magnus.

People thought we were crazy for having a baby in a tent, but we knew that hundreds of thousands of years of evolution had prepared us for survival without central heating and all the mod cons of daily life that we enjoy today. Even now, Magnus sleeps better outside in the fresh air than he does anywhere else.

Finding a balance between meeting the needs of a newborn son and a dog who was used to all of my attention 24/7 was not easy, but I made sure I showed Jet the same loyalty she had shown me since day one.

(*above*) I could not be prouder of Kate for how she handled her pregnancy and the way she grabbed motherhood by the horns, despite her challenging postpartum circumstances. She continued on, knowing deep down that she was giving her baby the best start possible.

(*right*) It's amazing what can come from following your heart.

The final day and the final mile. After an interview with Carol Vorderman,
it was time to finish this walk.

Our good friend Brian drove from Newcastle, armed with these wonderful flags.
Personally, this whole mile was one big blur. I was completely overwhelmed and
worried that it was too much for Jet. It was her one last little push and, even if I had
to carry her, if anyone deserved to cross that line with me, it was her.

now, it was easy to forget that our 'normal' of camping every night year-round was abnormal for others, especially when it came to places nobody else would dream of wanting to spend the night! From the layby, we scrambled over the barrier to a grassy area and found a knoll safely away from the road.

As I grabbed our gear from the boot of the car to hop over the road railing and erect the tent, I saw a beautiful embrace between father and daughter and noticed a few tears running down Ian's face as Kate reassured him that she'd be fine. To this day, I've never been sure if it was pride, or tears of concern and sadness! I have no doubt that neither Ian nor Val was aware of the power this walk was having on our veterans and other people that followed us, but I hoped at least one day they would understand that this wasn't just two people living in a tent walking around the coast, but much more than that. Ian was just being a protective father, concerned for Kate's wellbeing, and I understood that this could take some time.

We woke up eager and ready to go to meet Kate's friend Soph, her husband Alex and their three beautiful children, Teddy, Arthur and Olive. I know Kate was excited, as this was the first time she'd seen friends since starting the walk, plus she was Arthur's godmother. The night before, because of the heat in the tent at night-time, I'd taken off the long johns I always wore to avoid ticks or other unwanted beasties surrounding my undercarriage and legs – the first time that I'd ever done this! The next morning, I went outside and knelt on the grass looking over Whitby Bay while Kate got herself organized in the tent. As soon as she was done, without a second thought, I put my long johns on and we headed back in the car with Ian and Val for a spot of breakfast before meeting up with the Trings.

During breakfast I started to feel a strange tingling sensation around my legs and around the hamstrings. I said that I was going to the toilet and walked in to investigate the peculiar feeling. When I pulled my long johns down, I noticed that the area all around both my thighs had swollen terribly, with lumps all over my legs from the knee up – bites! I shit myself. *What on earth was this?* I thought.

Not wanting to make a drama or ruin what I knew would be a wonderful day for Kate, I kept my mouth shut. *I'll just deal with this later,* I thought, as we drove around with about 10 miles to go before we met up with Sophie and family. A big mistake. As I sat in the back of Ian's car with Jet nestled between Kate and me, my legs really started to itch. I pulled back my kilt to show Kate. 'What the hell is that?' she whispered.

'God knows!' I said. 'But I'll sort it later. Let's just have a nice day.'

As soon as we arrived, my general health started to decline rapidly. I felt incredibly shaky and very hot as we walked down to the nearby beach to meet Soph and family to do the old meet and greet. I felt dizzy and faint, and my vision was blurring, but I was determined to keep up appearances. I just cracked on. It would just be too ironic if this hardy guy Kate had spoken so much of to friends and family ended up hospitalized from some bites on the second day of meeting them.

As the hours went on, my breathing became much shallower and more frequent and it felt like my throat was closing over. I would keep making excuses that I drank too much water and needed to go to the toilet or I was off to get a can of Coke, but really I would just go around the corner out of sight, drop to my knees and start to panic. My swollen legs were now ballooning in size and turning a strange red-purple colour.

Eventually it became too much and I knew I was in trouble. I walked back and, as calmly and politely as possible, said to Kate, 'I don't feel very well and I really need to go!' She had no idea of the extremity of the situation, but by now I'd realized that I had been bitten and was having a massive allergic reaction. The only cause that sprung to mind, given where we were, was a false widow spider. I tried my best to make as little a fuss as possible, but, knowing very soon I could be heading into anaphylactic shock, I insisted we had to leave.

We parted ways with Sophie and family and made our way back up to the car, parked half a mile away up a huge hill. I plodded along with Jet, focusing on every stone, pebble or anything I could keep my eyes on so as not to pass out. Maybe I shouldn't have underplayed this as, when we got back to the car park, while I was desperate to get inside and be taken to the nearest chemist, Kate took a detour to go and barter with the ticket man to make sure we would be allowed back in again later now that we had paid for the day!

It was at this point that my tone of voice changed. 'Kate, I feel really fucking bad. I need to go!'

'Hang on,' she said.

'Kate!' I shouted. 'Let's go, now!' The drive back to Whitby felt like years with the constant feeling of my throat closing over. Then, to make matters worse, I started having a panic attack. I honestly thought I was going to die. There was Ian and Val expecting to meet a tough adventurer who never got ill, who had traversed unpaved mountains and survived winters in the most brutal places in a tent, and who was now being taken down by a fucking spider near Whitby. Typical.

As we got to Whitby and Ian sat waiting for a parking spot, it was all too much. I was shaking so badly that I could barely even open the door handle to get out of the car! Leaving Jet with Kate, Ian and Val, I stumbled into the chemist and dropped to my knees. I explained what I thought had happened and after hearing that my throat was closing over, they immediately called an ambulance. I was in a hell of a state. I managed to focus and find Piriton to bring down the allergic reaction. As I started to take one out of the box, to my utter disbelief, the chemist grabbed the box from me and said I'd have to pay for it first.

'Are you actually kidding me?' I mumbled. With that, I had to drag myself off my knees and tell her my PIN, as I was too shaky to press the buttons on the machine myself. I couldn't believe the inhumanity of it, given how much of a mess I was in. I took two tablets immediately, crunching them with my teeth to get them into my system. Around half an hour later and what seemed like a lifetime, the ambulance turned up. It was all a bit of a blur. They took me inside and gave me a shot of something and my symptoms began to reduce, but the paramedics were concerned and told me that my heart rate was ridiculous and I needed to rest for a week, as this was becoming very serious. I felt so grateful to the paramedics, without whom I wouldn't have lasted. I love people who spend their lives saving others; they really are the heart of our society.

That night, given the exceptional circumstances, Ian and Val offered to pay for a B&B for us so that I could try to recover, and we gratefully agreed. Jet lay by my side knowing something was up and giving me constant licks, while Kate took the piss out of me, knowing that's exactly what I wanted rather than sympathy! It wasn't the best first meeting of the parents, and I would say that my ego was a bit dented, but the next morning, I was raring and ready to go again. There wasn't a chance I'd be sitting it out for a week; we had coastline to walk and money to raise for charity.

I was very fortunate that this experience didn't completely finish me off, and how lucky I was to have not been in a place where I couldn't have received help! It's at times like this that it really hits home just how quickly something can go wrong and the seriousness of being alone while in the wilds. Thank God it happened here! Needless to say, I never went anywhere without my long johns again!

After Whitby, we headed down the coast through Scarborough, Filey, Bridlington, Hornsea and Withernsea. The coastline here had long, running stretches of mud cliffs that had formed when the last Ice Age pushed the mud into the sea. When it eventually melted, it had left miles and miles of brittle mud and stone cliffs that over time the sea had gotten its teeth into and eroded. Even in contemporary times, small towns and villages had fallen victim to the sea's wrath, along with caravan parks and houses that sit close to the edge. We were shocked at just how close many of the properties were to being completely washed away and lost to the sea for ever.

Without knowledge of the tides, mud cliffs can be an incredibly dangerous place to be walking below. Walking at high tide would leave no beach, meaning that if we weren't careful, we'd get cut off by the sea at the bottom of the cliffs. Landslides happened frequently, and we'd constantly discover old pillboxes from the Second World War half submerged in sand and mud. As the tide went out, it gave us a clear indication of just how much our coastline had eroded even since the war. A scary thought and no doubt one of the reasons houses in this area are much cheaper, given that there's a strong possibility in your lifetime that you may well lose your home to the sea, as many had done before.

Walking the East Riding of Yorkshire towards Withernsea, we had a few weeks of incredibly uncomfortable nights as our roll mat had punctured once again. With no money and no means to replace it, we would spend night after night sleeping on the hard floor. I'd always remind Kate that it could be worse – at least it was mid-August! In Shetland, I'd spent a month in the winter sleeping on the floor without a roll mat and it was brutal. But, still, it takes its toll in any season. By now, we were getting tired and were direly in need of a full night's kip without the constant tossing and turning to find comfort.

We received a message from a lady called Sarah as we approached Withernsea, who offered to put us up in a small shed full of hay bales in which to spend a few nights if we liked. Sleeping on hay bales offered some sort of comfort and sounded like just the ticket, and we leaped at the idea. It would save us having to put up the tent for a few nights and, better still, we'd be able to use a running tap for water rather than having to carry so much. Sarah and her daughter Beth picked us up on the coast just before Withernsea and took us to a small stronghold in the midst of an acre of land with a wooden stable occupied by their pride and joy – two beautiful horses. Directly next to it was a wooden shed filled waist-height with hay bales that would be our home for a couple of nights! Perfect.

It was now August 2021 and only a few days before Kate's thirty-fifth birthday. While we were staying in Sarah's shed, we would walk during the day with only water to carry and leave our bags back in the shed. At the end of our walking day, Sarah would pick us up and bring us back to the stables, cooking up an array of hearty dinners each night to feast on beside the horses. Inside, the shed was riddled with some rather sizeable spiders that at some point during the night would be crawling all over us, but we'd gotten so used to this by now. I knew that they would cause no harm, unless of course they happened to be my new nemesis – false widows! But I'd already checked that and was satisfied we were all clear on that front. It was only a few good old common house spiders crawling in and around us.

Meanwhile, with the help of Michelle, a lady from Hull who followed the journey, I had arranged to surprise Kate for her birthday with a romantic outside meal. With Kate distracted inside the shed, Michelle arrived to help me set up a gazebo with fairy lights, a table, candles, a bottle of bubbly, and a wonderful homemade spaghetti bolognese with all the trimmings. In no way can I take any of the credit for the effort that was made – all I had to do was set it up and Michelle did the rest! I really couldn't have been more grateful for the effort she put in, and our evening was wonderful. We toasted Kate's thirty-fifth year on Planet Earth under the gazebo strung with beautiful lights and enjoyed a hearty meal, knowing the hay bales we would sleep on that night offered far more protection and comfort than the ground. I couldn't afford a birthday present, and Kate's never bothered about gifts, but never mind that, because the next day Kate was about to receive a gift beyond measure.

14

Blue lines!

The following morning, we got up early, ready to put a good shift in. We wanted to make the most of weight-free walking and to get through Withernsea and down the coast as far as our new base. Before we set off, Kate mentioned that she still hadn't got her period, which was now around three weeks late. She'd picked up a pregnancy test and, although it had only been a month ago that we first discussed trying for a baby, she decided to give it a quick go before we left, just for peace of mind's sake. Not for a moment did either of us expect it to turn out positive.

Kate knelt on top of the bales that were our bed and weed into one of my titanium cooking pots on top of the pregnancy test. All the while, I was thinking, *If you miss the pot, you're sleeping on that side!* Once she'd finished, she handed me the pregnancy test and we waited.

'Sorry, mate, not this time,' I said to Kate when only the one blue line was showing. We'd expected that anyway and both laughed it off. About to grab my jacket and set off, I took another look at the pregnancy test for good measure. I think I stopped breathing for a few seconds.

'Dude,' I said. 'You're not going to believe this: you're pregnant!'

Kate looked at me rather sternly, as if to say, *This is not a very funny wind-up.*

'I'm serious, Kate, have a look! There's two lines! Honey, we're going to have a baby!'

Kate grabbed the pregnancy test and saw for herself. I think she was temporarily stunned, just in pure shock to begin with that this could happen so quickly.

I joked: 'What do you expect with such pedigree sperm!'

We both chuckled and embraced in the most loving hug. I would say we didn't believe it and thought maybe there was something wrong with the test, but if I'm truthful, deep down, I knew it was right.

It was a lovely day walking through Withernsea, and the weather being slightly overcast made for a cooler day and much easier for Jet. Kate was still unable to believe the news and decided to pick up a few more pregnancy tests. From behind various bushes and public toilets around Withernsea she ended up doing five tests that day, and all agreed – we were pregnant!

Having a baby had been something that we'd discussed, and we both agreed that we would rather have it while we were still in the UK instead of on a likely more extreme adventure abroad after completing the walk. Not for one second did either of us consider how we were going to make this work; we just enjoyed the moment and cherished the fact that we had cemented our love for each other for ever. It was the most wonderful news, and I knew Kate was going to be the best mum any child could ask for. Inside Kate's belly, our little adventurer was starting to grow. I was now truly the most complete and happy man alive. That night as Kate lay sleeping, I rested my hand on her belly and cried.

I thought about Caitlin and, although she grew up to be the most amazing daughter a father could ask for, I still couldn't shake the feeling that I'd let her down, and it still hurt. But now I'd been given a second chance, and I would never make that same mistake again. Now older, wiser and for the first time in my life finally content, I made a promise to myself that this little baby would have the best father anyone could ask for. *Thank you, Kate*, I thought to myself, *I love you so much*. I closed my eyes and went to sleep feeling content.

Like many parents to be, Kate and I had decided to keep the news to ourselves until later in the pregnancy when it was too obvious to hide. It was still early days and we just felt it was the right thing to do, especially now that we were in the limelight as somewhat public figures. We didn't make any real plans or worry too much about it. I can imagine that most in our position would've retired from the walk, found a family home and got jobs to start bringing some money in. And quite understandably so. We also had plenty of people tell us that of course that's what we would have to do now. But we loved this adventure we were on and felt differently. What better way for a baby to grow inside of a mother than one who is constantly outside in the fresh air, exercising daily, eating healthily and totally absorbed in nature. In our eyes, it was a win-win! Kate was determined to keep going because that's who she is, but she also believed it would be the best thing for her and the baby. The walk would continue exactly as it had, and our mindset was to just take each day as it came, as we always had.

It was at this point that I finally agreed to sign a contract with book publisher Pan Macmillan to write my first ever book. I was spurred on by the thought that we'd soon need a proper income to bring up a child. We both had complete faith that once this adventure was over, by hook or by crook, we would find a way to make a living and keep pursuing our dreams. We would just take it one step at a time, one day at a time, crossing any obstacles as we went – it's just how we rolled! We had no idea how we were going to make it all work; we just knew that we would.

Soon enough we were met with a stroke of good fortune when a message came through on Instagram from Ben Fogle. It turned out he had been following my adventures for some time and he had seen that we were in and around an area where he would soon be doing a talk on his live tour, so he got in touch to ask if we would like to come and see him speak. He even offered to treat us to a meal beforehand.

I'm not a fan of the word 'envy', because I'm a firm believer that you get out what you put into life, but it's fair to say that Ben has my dream job. Travelling all around the world doing exciting things every day, meeting different types of people from all walks of life and exploring beautiful landscapes. Comparing what you have with others can be a dangerous game, and not one I've ever been interested in playing, but I really respect the way Ben had carved a path for himself that allows him to pursue his dreams.

Kate and I were definitely excited to meet him and hear about his adventures because he came across as a very genuine, friendly, hardworking guy. We listened to his talk, during which he gave us all a big shout-out, and realized that the respect was mutual – he'd made it quite clear that despite his own accomplishments, he was not only fascinated by what we were doing but keen to champion our efforts from his own platform.

When we met him in the flesh, he didn't disappoint. There was something authentic and earnest about him; you couldn't help but like Ben. We agreed to stay in touch.

Back on the walk, we were soon to reach Lincolnshire, Norfolk, Suffolk and then into Essex towards London. Crossing these counties would take us through the rest of the summer, autumn and into winter. It was always a relief to finish the summer given the logistics with Jet. People always expect winter to be by far the hardest time of year and, my word, it could indeed be brutal at times, but summer could be just as tough.

Our timing with the seasons and the terrain also seemed to be working out well given Kate's pregnancy. The majority of this stretch of Lincolnshire coastline was made up of incredibly flat marshland walking, and all along raised footpaths a few feet tall on the banks, with running grassy slopes either side keeping us well above the boggy marshland, which was much less taxing for her. The sea almost always out of sight, especially on a low tide, but it was great for wildlife like seals and birds who thrived off the nutrients lurking beneath the sandy mud. We found ourselves walking along the banks of marshes day after day, punctuated by the odd town such as Boston and Skegness (or Costa del Skeg as it's nicknamed), with its abundance of caravans, coastal bars and, of course, Butlin's!

At times, I would joke with Kate that certain sections where we could literally see in a straight line for miles were like Route 66 in America; it felt like we weren't even moving! It's not really my type of walking if I'm honest; I prefer the more extreme end of the scale, but it made it easier-going for Kate, who was sailing through her first trimester with no sickness or feeling in any way pregnant! We would often comment that maybe this had a lot to do with the healthy fresh air, and all-round active and healthy lifestyle. She could've just been very lucky of course, but I prefer to think the former.

While we were navigating the Suffolk coastline and camped up for the evening about to get our food on, an old friend turned up out of the blue.

Way back on the west coast of Scotland, while navigating my way around the Hebridean Uists in winter, I had to return back down to Northamptonshire, England, for the funeral of an immediate family member. By pure luck, it just so happened somebody in the Uists was heading down that way and could give me a lift. Quite unreal, now I come to think about it. After the funeral, I put out a post to test the powers of social media to see if I could somehow pepper pot my way back up to Scotland, catching lifts with whomever I could. I ended up making yet another lifelong friend with a gentleman called Steve, who did an eight-hour overnight drive all the way from the Midlands up to the Isle of Skye, where I could return to the Uists via ferry. It was a huge ask and quite frankly I couldn't believe that someone would go out of their way to do something so kind!

I think it's safe to say that Steve and I cemented a bond in the time it took us to drive to Skye. He was open and honest about some issues he'd had that had turned him to drink; little did I know, but at the time, Steve was not personally in a good way, and my being honest about my problems definitely helped him! And when Steve dropped me off on the Isle of Skye ready for the immediate return journey, he was adamant that if there was anything I needed throughout the rest of this journey, he would be there to help.

It was the first time I'd seen him since we'd met three years ago, and he turned up in his blue Volkswagen van to say hello and offer any assistance needed – an incredible gesture given the fact that he actually lived in Birmingham and had driven all of this way on the off-chance that he might find us! Kate was nine weeks pregnant by now and we needed to get her back to Gloucestershire for scans and various other baby checks. Upon hearing this, Steve sat us down and was adamant that he didn't care where it was, what time it was, and how short notice it would be – if we needed a lift, he would be the one to come pick us up, take us to the appointment and then drop us back to the stage of the coast that we had left off. From the word go, I really liked Steve, not just because of the favours he was doing us, but because he was honest and real, noble attributes that are a hard thing to find in a person these days. And, true to his word, from the very first scan through to the very end of Kate's pregnancy, Steve was always there for us; he wanted no money, no thanks, but just to do a good deed for people that he liked and admired. He is one of life's true earth angels, although he would never accept that.

While walking Essex, we would pass through Colchester, once my home and the base for two battalions of the Parachute Regiment, 2 and 3 Para. I was bowled over when a soldier I went through training and served with, named Scotty, now an officer who'd worked his way through the ranks from being a private, got in touch for the first time since I'd left the Forces, asking if I'd be happy to come and do a talk in front of the Paras about my adventure. I must be honest: I was slightly nervous, as it'd been a long time and, like many soldiers after leaving, I'd had very little contact – if any – with my old friends. That's just life. But it would be a huge honour. It's incredible to see what a friend looks like having known him all those years ago, and when we finally met it was like we had seen each other just yesterday, even if we'd both aged twenty years since then!

Scotty took us into camp and into the Sergeant's Mess, where I was made aware of friends who had sadly passed in combat while serving in the Middle East. It really hit me hard, but I was so proud and happy to see that my old friend Scotty had made a great career for himself. When I'd done my talk, I was invited up to say hello to the commanding officer, which is a big deal in such an elite force as the Paras. With Kate and Jet by my side, the CO did something that I will cherish and hold dear to me for the rest of my life. As he shook my hand and thanked me for what I was doing for the armed forces, and for being such a great advocate for the Parachute Regiment, our palms touched, and I felt a silver coin being passed from his hand to mine. It was the CO's Coin of Excellence, something that few people ever receive – awarded to those in recognition of their consid- erable efforts to be a force for good within the armed forces. And it had been given to me by a man who had reached the pinnacle of the British Army, commanding officer of the best elite force in the world, and a senior officer in the British special forces, the SAS. To say this was an honour was an understatement. I felt in no way that I deserved this, and still don't! But it meant a lot to have received this.

That evening after I'd left, I sat alone for a while, thinking about my time in the Paras, friends I no longer spoke to, friends I'd lost, and friends that I had rekindled relationships with. I shed a little tear, and once again reminded myself what a special thing I had once been a part of, and how honoured I was to receive such a commendation for my time served and, more so, for the efforts I was putting in now to help my fellow family members of the armed forces. I will take that coin with me to the grave.

15

Bottled in Basildon

One morning, while camped up just shy of Mersea Island, and having just come from Colchester, we were going through our normal morning routine. I was outside getting the coffee on and trying to give my pregnant Kate a much-deserved rest in the tent. She was cuddled up with Jet, both keeping warm together as it was now December, and all of a sudden I heard her call me in a quiet, serious voice.

'Hang on, babe, two seconds,' I replied as I took the coffee off the gas stove and made my way back to the tent.

'Have a feel here,' said Kate as she rubbed Jet's under-belly. 'Chris, I think she has another lump.'

I dropped my coffee and knelt in the entrance of the tent to inspect her. Kate wasn't wrong. 'That's two in the space of under a year,' I said, trying my best to hold back tears so Jet didn't see me upset! I slumped onto my backside and sat facing away from the tent, fearing the worst, knowing that the last lump had been cancerous. Then I made a phone call.

Back in Scotland, not too far from the border, the breakfast show *This Morning* had asked if we would do a feature for a segment called 'Furiends', which told heart-warming stories about the connection between dogs and humans, particularly over lockdown. They sent up a camera crew along with the Australian vet Dr Scott Miller. While filming for the feature, Kate and I really warmed to Scott. He had spent a lifetime working with animals and we could really see his passion and love for all creatures great and small. He is a genuine, lovely man and we were touched at how quickly he connected with Jet over the course of the morning. We kept each other's numbers after the filming and promised to keep in touch. And we did exactly that! Scott would always assure me that if there was anything we ever needed regarding Jet, or even just any advice, that he was always at the end of the phone. So, when we discovered the second lump on Jet, I phoned Scott without hesitation, asking what our best course of action would be.

By pure coincidence, Scott had been meaning to get in touch with us about the possibility of doing a feature for a show he films in Australia called *Bondi Vets*. After a short discussion, we arranged that Scott would come and meet us on Mersea Island to film for the day and the following morning we would go to Richmond, Surrey, where his vet practice is located, for Jet to undergo yet another operation to remove the lump. Amazingly, he offered to do the operation completely free of charge! Having spoken quite a few times and seen me with Jet, he knew how much she meant to me and gave me his word that he would look after her as well as he possibly could. I trusted him and was happy with the arrangement.

A week later, we met up with Scott on Mersea Island to start filming. I was quite tired with worry by this point. Jet was as much a part of my family as anyone. I was so nervous, but knew she was in amazing hands. I remember standing on the beach while being asked questions in front of the camera and, out of the corner of my eye, seeing Scott kneel on the floor next to Jet, having a good feel at what we had discovered. Naturally, my mind had gone completely off track of what was being asked in front of the camera. I knew this would be aired in front of millions of Australians, but, having been asked similar questions so many times, I went into autopilot while I focused on Scott's hands in my peripheral vision to try to read his expression and get a clue as to how worried I should be.

After a full day of filming, we ended the last section next to our tent, near a small pond on the north side of the island. With the cameras rolling and Scott about to tell us what we thought we already knew, I was confident I'd be fine; knowing that she had a lump was something that I'd already accepted in the week building up to filming, or at least that's what I thought. Standing between me and Kate, and with Jet lying on the floor enjoying the warmth of the sun, looking as beautiful as ever and completely unaware of the situation, he said to me with a camera recording, 'Chris, I know how much you love this dog and I want you to know that we're going to do everything in our power to make sure that she's going to be okay, but I'm sorry to say that the lump that you felt is actually one of six that I found lying deeper under the skin.' I might as well have been standing in the centre of a black hole! Everything around me kept moving but my whole world just suddenly stood perfectly still, silent and breathless. Then collapsed.

I looked at Kate, her eyes welling up, knowing damn well the impact the news was having on me, but, given how much she also loved Jet, it was breaking her heart too. Scott put his arm on my shoulder and said, 'Chris, are you okay, mate?'

'Of course I'm not fucking okay!' I felt like saying, but I nodded my head as tears ran down my face. At that moment, Jet got up and walked in my direction.

'Chris,' Scott said quietly, 'she's coming over because she can see you're upset. This is where you must be strong and try your very hardest to not let her see or even know what she's about to take on. I can honestly say in all my years as a vet, I've never seen a better bond between a dog and a human than I have with you and Jet.

'It's a big operation and I have to tell you that there is no guarantee given the scale of the operation that she will get through this, but I promise you, if there's a chance, I will make it happen.' And then he wrapped his arms around me.

I had to walk it off to regain my composure while Kate took one for the team and continued chatting to Scott. Kate and I were broken-hearted, but this fight was not over yet! A healthy lifestyle and incredible fitness would work in Jet's favour if she was to pull through. Before Scott left and with the camera no longer rolling, he explained that older female dogs that haven't been spayed are also more susceptible to cancer, so he would also perform this sterilization at the same time as the surgery to remove the cancerous lumps. Incredibly grateful yet so distraught, we jumped into a hire car that Scott had gotten for us and we started making our way down to Richmond for the operation the following morning.

Seeing as we'd left so late in the day, we decided to stop off just outside of London and then leave early in the morning to avoid London traffic. We'd been put up in a hotel smack bang in the centre of Basildon, and, both exhausted and stricken with worry, we made our way up to the room. As much as I tried, I just couldn't get the idea out of my head that something might go wrong, and it would be the last night I would cuddle up with Jet. I simply couldn't process it. Memories of me and her together, and all the things we had done, flashed through my mind like a film reel. I needed a few minutes to myself, and seeing as Kate and I were both hungry, I made my way out of the hotel and towards a Wagamama's.

I'd never been in this area before, and to me, it was like a miniature version of Las Vegas, but with youths hanging around outside the arcades, while adults walked past, keeping their heads down, avoiding any trouble. I thought to myself, *What on earth has it come to when fully grown adults are scared of teenagers?*

As I returned to the hotel with dinner in either hand to take back to Kate, some kids in their late teens/early twenties started taking the piss out of my attire, calling me some rather unsavoury names. Continuing to walk past them, I smiled and said, 'Come on, lads, we're all friends here. Have a nice evening,' before continuing on my way. Before I knew it, a glass bottle struck the back of my head and smashed. The impact put me on my knees, though I'd had enough experience in my life to know you needed to stay focused on something so as not to pass out after being struck.

I put my hands on the back of my head to check for any gashes. I was incredibly lucky that the glass bottle had hit me in such a way that it shattered all around me. Already there was a huge egg of a lump, but no blood. I got back up to my feet and turned to see passers-by stood watching, making no attempt to stop the four lads now sprinting off and getting away scot-free. It was at this point that I had to remind myself that my Para days were long gone, and any urge to chase them down and let them know they'd just picked on the wrong person was not an option. I had a pregnant girlfriend and a dog just about to go into surgery waiting for me, and the hotel was only a few hundred yards away.

Concussed and shaken, I grabbed the bags of food, which unbeknown to me had split at the bottom, meaning as I walked, the food was being spilled everywhere as I made my way up to the hotel. When I arrived, I was white as a ghost and shaking with rage at those little fuckers who had gotten away with impunity. I already had anxiety, having hardly slept, and knowing that I might be saying goodbye to my best friend tomorrow. I was a complete mess.

'I'm so sorry, Kate,' I said. 'I'll be okay in a minute. I don't want you to get stressed for our baby. Let's just go to bed.' I didn't sleep a wink that night.

The next morning, we jumped into the hire car as I showed Kate the shattered glass on the ground where I'd been hit. Deep inside me, something was wrong; I had impaired vision, my fists were constantly clenched and clammy, my breathing shallow. From experience, I knew that tiredness, overwhelming worry about Jet, and the fact I was back in a place where other people's actions could sap away at me meant that the happy energy that I had held onto so tightly was now in jeopardy! In a nutshell, I hadn't felt this unhappy for a very long time. Riddled with the almightiest panic attack, we headed down to Richmond for what could potentially be the worst day of my life.

16

Under the knife:
Jet's surgery

I had to ask Kate to pull over a few times so I could catch
my breath as we made our way down to Scott's veterinary
surgery. Before we went in she looked at me and said,
'Chris, you look like total shit. Are you okay?!'

'I just wanna get out of here as soon as possible,' I
replied. 'Let's get this done.'

Jet excitedly wagged her tail, as ever looking at me with
an expression that said, *What's next, Dad?* I put her on
the lead and we took her in. With the cameras up and
ready to go, Scott made his appearance from the surgery
upstairs, took one look at me and said, 'Jet, I'm not sure
who I should be more worried about, you or your dad!
Are you alright, mate?' he asked me.

With a quick nod and already holding back the tears,
I said rather bluntly, 'I'm fine. Thank you for doing this.'

Knowing mine and Jet's bond, before the camera started rolling Scott came over to me and said, 'Chris, I know how she'll be if you're not with her, and we would never normally do this, but for you, I will. When we put Jet under the anaesthetic, I want you to be the last thing she sees before she goes under.'

My brain consumed itself with anxiety and fears of the worst, and all while being in front of a camera. I just tried to pretend it wasn't there. I lifted Jet up onto the operating table as Scott and his crew prepared themselves, all the while constantly talking to her, telling her, 'It's okay, buddy. I'll see you in a minute.' As Scott injected the anaesthetic needle into my girl, she looked directly into my eyes as she slowly but surely fell asleep.

I left the room and made my way upstairs, where Kate took my hand and guided me outside for a walk. My panic attack had taken on such a force that I couldn't move, however, and we would spend the next four hours of Jet's surgery sat in a car outside the practice. It was the longest and worst four hours of my life. No matter what Kate said, nothing helped. The last time I felt this broken was before I started to walk. All I could do was think back to Hildasay, watching Jet run around, free and happy.

When one of Scott's colleagues came out to the car, I held my breath for the news.

'Chris,' she said, 'Scott said can you come down now, but be aware Jet really isn't in a good way after such a heavy dose of anaesthetic, and of course the operation. It's too early to tell, but she has come through the oper- ation and is still with us. Again, Scott would never normally let anyone down at this stage, but Jet is pining for you and so we are happy for you to come in if you don't mind seeing her in this way.'

I sprinted down the stairs to see Jet lying there making the most awful noises you would ever wish to hear your dog utter. She was wrapped in a huge blue bandage that covered her entire torso, with blood coating the underneath, and I fell to my knees in the small cubicle and wrapped myself around her, talking to her and letting her know that I was here. Jet had saved me, and it was my turn to repay the favour.

Still suffering from blurred vision and consumed with a panic attack, I refused to let anybody else carry Jet back upstairs. By this point I was a complete and utter mess! When we got into the main room of the practice, I just asked if we could just go home. Scott filled me in with a few details, along with the medication she would need, and said, 'The best thing you can do now is let her rest for as long as possible, a minimum of six weeks.'

'Scott,' I said, 'if it means I have to stop the walk, that's exactly what I will do. She's my girl!'

'I know, mate,' he replied. 'She couldn't be in better hands.'

We had arranged to go back to Kate's mum Liz's house in Malvern for the duration of Jet's recovery, knowing there was still a chance her body might not react well to the operation. It was going to be a long few weeks! We started the three-hour journey back to Malvern with Kate driving and me in the back of the car with Jet, talking to her the entire way. While Jet was in theatre,

I had kept looking at the car's back seat, hoping with all that I had that she would be in that same seat as we returned back to Malvern. And I reminded myself how lucky we were that she was here as I'd wished, even if her condition wasn't great.

We arrived back at Kate's mum's in Colwall in the Malvern Hills late that evening. I was slightly worried about taking Jet there, as Liz is incredibly houseproud, and the idea of Jet's blood dripping on her carpets and on the bedsheets was a bit of a worry. But she couldn't have been more welcoming and understanding. She had met us a few times previously and formed a lovely bond with both Jet and me, and I will always be grateful for how she responded to our difficulty. Knowing how much Jet meant to me, Liz went above and beyond to make everything as comfortable for her as possible. For the next week, I'm quite sure I didn't leave Jet's side once. The anaesthetic had worn off, so she was in pronounced pain, but more pressing was the ever-present struggle to get painkillers and anti-inflammatories inside her, despite them being disguised in dog treats or chunks of butter!

Kate, now visibly pregnant, was around the whole time, bringing me up breakfast, lunch and dinner every single day and coming in to lie with Jet so I could walk around the room and stretch my legs. It was a really intense week, with endless mornings, afternoons and evenings of cleaning her wounds, which stretched from her private parts, across her upper stomach and into her rib cage. It was an awful process that had to be done, but I would remind myself how grateful I was that she was fighting this, that her body had not given up.

Throughout this period she was having to be carried up and down the stairs a few times a day, as she struggled so hard to even do a wee – never mind a number two – due to the pain and freshness of her wounds. Then, about four weeks after the surgery, something incredible happened.

Kate called from downstairs, asking me to pop down and have a look at something, so I gave Jet a kiss on the ear and told her I'd be back in a few seconds. As I made my way towards the staircase, I heard a thud and turned around, hoping Jet hadn't fallen off the bed. But, to my complete surprise, there she stood behind me, her tail waggling! I dropped down to my knees and put my arms around her neck to give her a gentle cuddle. I was almost annoyed that she had jumped off the bed, potentially reopening her wounds, which were held together by staples at this point, but at the same time, it was the first sign that my walking partner and best buddy was on the mend. She was going to pull through!

'Jet, my friend,' I said to her as her tail continued to wag, 'I thought I was going to lose you, pal! How stupid of me! You're a force to be reckoned with.'

Slowly but surely, day by day and week by week, her strength started to come back, and full recovery was imminent! Dr Scott Miller had saved my girl's life! There are some things in life that people do for you where you will simply never be able to repay the favour, and that man will have a place in my heart for ever. It took about two months in total for Jet to fully recover – and once again do zoomies in the back garden at Kate's mum's.

We waited a little while longer before we brought Jet back out on the walk, knowing it was going to be slow progress. But the main thing was, our girl was still with us. With the team now back to full strength, we were ready to continue our adventures around the UK coastline. It was yet another little reminder to both me and Kate, how precious and fragile life can be, and how grateful we were to have our health. Soon it would be time to prepare ourselves for another little life to join our team – things were looking up again! I was so happy Jet was going to be around for the arrival of our baby, who would have her to play with as a big sister.

17

Rest is a yurt in Ringstead Bay

After we returned to Mersea Island in Essex (our last stop on the walk), with Jet now fully recovered, we made our way around London towards the coast, through Margate, Broadstairs, Ramsgate, Deal and then over the White Cliffs of Dover! There were a few built-up areas as we headed round to Ramsgate, but generally, this stretch was easy walking – predominantly marsh ground and still very flat. I kept such a close eye on Jet as we went around these parts, even though she had recovered to the best of any dog's ability. After the level of surgery she'd undergone, I think it's safe to say that she didn't have the same spring in her step as she'd had pre-operation. Her wounds had by now completely healed and all in all she was still the happy little sniffing dog I'd always known, but she would tire more quickly now. I'd already noticed her slowing down over the previous year and I had to admit to myself that she was getting older.

Knowing how far we had left to go of the walk, this started to become a regular worry on my mind. I was constantly going through ideas in my head about how we could retire Jet earlier, yet still be able to continue walking ourselves. Believe me when I say, we tried so hard with Jet's cart, which I'd bought on eBay, and specially adapted with handles so it could be attached directly to my backpack and I could pull her along. I dragged it over cliffs and carried it over stiles, but she refused to even go inside. She was adamant and having none of it!

The bottom line was that all Jet knew was to be walking by my side, and that's all she wanted. Try as we might to tow her in a dog cart, it was proving futile, and I just had to accept that this wasn't going to happen. Our efforts finally came to a standstill on the White Cliffs of Dover, when the cart broke, and I had to carry it for miles over my head on the uphill inclines. I trusted that at some point I would devise a new plan, but until then it was just a simple case of having to slow down and only walk the mileage that old Jet could manage.

Kate continued to be an absolute machine! While pregnant, she had walked the Yorkshire, Lincolnshire, Norfolk, Suffolk, Essex and now Kent coast – six counties, nearly all of it sleeping in a tent. Her due date was 23 April, so she was now eight months pregnant, and I noticed that getting out of the tent each morning had started to become more and more of a mission as each week passed. The grunts and groans of pulling herself from the floor were getting too much for me to behold, and certainly too much for her, as the weight of her stomach made things very difficult – not to mention the number of times she was now having to get up and out of her sleeping bag to pee in the night!

She would never moan about it, and it wasn't until I saw her almost in tears one morning waking up in the tent, which was pitched on a garage floor. As we neared Hastings, I knew it was time for Kate to get some much-needed comfort. Kate will never know how many times, when we were walking or just sitting there taking in the view on a clifftop, and even sometimes when she was asleep, that I would watch her in complete awe! *What a woman you are*, I would think. Here she was, eight and a half months pregnant, still sleeping on a roll mat in a tent, having just been through yet another winter without a single gripe or ever once asking for more comfort beyond a hot-water bottle!

How on earth she was doing this, I will never know. It's one thing to be moving from place to place each and every day, never knowing where you're going to be sleeping, but the strength of mind it takes to know that you're going to be doing this day in, day out, in all weathers for the foreseeable future really takes a certain kind of person. By this point, Kate had been on the walk for almost two years, and I knew there were so many women out there that could take inspiration from her. She is the most determined person I know, and I can tell you, having known a load of Paras and having spent nearly five years walking the coastline myself by this point, that's quite something!

She never faltered when it came to doing what she believed was best for our baby – eating healthily, getting plenty of exercise and fresh air, even hanging upside down off coastal path benches to try to move the baby into position, which was breeching at this point, and doing yoga outside the tent at night. She never felt sorry for herself, never moaned about how tough it was; she just got on with it, singing terrible boyband numbers to me as we walked, or busting out history videos about the places we walked through, always with that upbeat, infectious smile of hers.

It was these attributes that had attracted me to Kate in the first place. I could sit and write about it all day, but unless you were witness to her, it's impossible to convey how strong-willed and determined this lady is that I'm so proud to call my girlfriend. A lot of the attention had been taken off Kate given the circumstances with Jet recently, and never once did she ask for more. However, I knew that it was now time to put all our focus and energy into making sure she was comfortable and ready for the most important and amazing moment of her life (other than meeting me of course!) . . . having our baby!

One thing that really struck me was that the further south we trekked, the more insular people became. Hellos or simple waves, which we had been so used to dishing out and receiving while walking around Scotland and the northeast of England, now seemed to become less and less frequent. We even started getting some strange looks and quite often heard people muttering under their breath as they walked past, 'What the hell is he wearing?' By the time we reached the Thames Estuary in and around London, it started to feel like we just weren't wanted: builders, youths and people in cars would often hurl abuse as they passed; whether it was because they thought we were homeless or just the fact that we really stood out from everyone else, we didn't know, but it really started to wear me down.

When it came to raising money for SSAFA, we'd found that media attention had become less and less. I felt that my efforts walking the west and north coast and the islands of Scotland over three years paled in comparison to Kate's achievement of sleeping homeless through winter while pregnant. And all this in a country where we weren't allowed fires and constantly had to sneak about to find a camp spot, often getting confronted and moved on. We hoped her steely determination would draw in more donations and looked forward to watching our fundraising target total grow. However, barely a single donation was being made for all our efforts for months on end, which was really deflating. What more could we be doing? If this didn't warrant a donation, then what would?

For the first time in my walk, I questioned whether our travails were worth it. But we couldn't stop now, so close to the end. Don't get me wrong: people were still being incredibly kind. We regularly received messages via social media offering garages, man sheds, caravans and even houses to stay in as we passed through Essex and Kent. Once we arrived in London, however, not a single offer was thrown our way. This may sound entitled, but it's just that when this generosity that you've been used to for so long suddenly stops, I couldn't help but wonder why on earth this was!

As each week passed, I had a growing sense of urgency to just get this walk done. But it was never going to be that simple: we still had huge logistical challenges of getting Jet to the end and, of course, the imminent question of how we were going to navigate ourselves around the south and southwest coast of England with a newborn baby, and eventually head back up into Wales! None of the challenges the walk had thrown my way throughout the journey up until now would come close to what lay ahead.

When I was in the brutal wilds of Scotland, I'd chuckled at how physically easy I'd find the southwest coast path. What I hadn't foreseen was that we were just about to enter sections of coast where pretty much everything, bar fresh air, had been monetized. The camping laws became even stricter, and it simply wasn't a place for a wild-living, nomadic walking family like ours.

Around three weeks before Kate's due date, we'd made it around Kent's coastline and arrived just outside Hastings. It had been a long and tedious slog to get to this point. We had been given a small building, much like a works office on a farm, by a gentleman called David, who was a veteran himself, and we soon discovered he was actually a relative of Kate's that she never knew about. One evening, I put the roll matt down, ready for Jet and me to settle on for the night, as it simply wouldn't take the weight of the three of us, with a fully grown baby inside Kate! There was a small leather sofa where Kate said she would prefer to sleep the night, and as I made her evening cup of herbal tea, she nestled down onto it. It wasn't long enough for her to stretch out, so her legs were slightly bent, and she had a cushion between them to ease her discomfort at night.

I looked at her as she closed her eyes, her belly hanging over the edge of the sofa, and I experienced a feeling of real guilt. I walked over to where the kettle was boiling and sat down for a second. *Mate*, I said to myself, *your girl carrying your baby is sleeping on a hard leather sofa with her belly hanging over the edge. It's time to step up and put a pause on the walk.* With that, I went back to Kate and knelt beside her.

'Kate, darling, I know this may not be what you want to do, and I don't want to come across as bossy, but there's no way in this world you're sleeping on that after tonight! I'm stopping the walk for us to go and have our baby!'

Kate nodded in agreement. I sensed relief from her and a personal admission that now was the time to stop. That aside, she'd received communication from the home-birth midwifery team in Dorchester. We'd planned for Kate to use a birthing pool inside a yurt to have the baby, and we were advised that we needed to be in the area from the 37-week mark.

Once again, our good friend Dan Davies, our master of sand arts, had come up to shoot some footage of us as we walked this final stretch, pre-baby, for our own memories. With the little money that we had left from getting paid for my last documentary, we hired a car and immediately took Kate to the comfort of a bed in the place where we'd arranged to have the baby – a yurt on the Dorset coast by Ringstead Bay. It was now time to bring our little adventurer into the world and expand our family. For now, the walk could wait.

The yurt was on the outskirts of Dorchester in the estate of a historic family home called Moignes Court. It had beautiful grounds surrounded by woodland and fields. The land immediately surrounding the house had been turned into a community area where people would rent either a yurt or an old, converted bus that had been turned into a simple homestead. From my understanding, the inhabitants would pay a small amount of rent and in return put in manual hours to help with the upkeep of the grounds and look after the land they were living on. It seemed to run well, and we soon met the other very friendly members of this community, most of whom were single mums with young children.

The soon-to-be inheritor of the beautiful estate, Ralph Cree, ran the place and was constantly working to keep the stately home maintained along with the surrounding land. He was another man of few words and very pleasant! Ralph and his wife home-schooled their two boys and I loved watching him play on the trampoline with them whenever he could. I admired him – the second he put down tools, he would go outside and have fun with the kids regardless of how tired he was. It got me excited knowing that in a few years, I'd be doing the same with my own, and that was the reason we were here.

Kate and I had been put in a yurt that sat not too far from the main house. She hoped to have a water birth inside the yurt, and we were so grateful to Jo and Helen, two lovely midwives from Becoming Families in Worcestershire, for giving us a birthing pool. While Jet had been recovering from her operation, these ladies had come to Kate's mum's house to give us three antenatal classes, as Kate had been unable to attend any before this point. I fully respected Kate's birthing plan choices but I knew that when the time came, I was genuinely going to have my hands full getting that birthing pool ready in the yurt, that much was for sure!

With help from Ralph, I got to work fastening water pipes together with attachments so that we had a pipe long enough to reach the birthing pool in the yurt. We made another fixture to fasten a hose to a hot-water tap that we could run directly from the house through the kitchen window to the pool, as the pool has to be maintained at 38 degrees for delivery of a baby. With a couple of mock runs, we decided that the pipe was working and stored it ready for the main event. Once Kate's waters had broken, it would be all systems go to get that pool filled and at the right temperature, while also trying to be there for Kate. I was completely ready to do my bit, which was obviously nothing in comparison to what Kate would be doing, but I did wonder at times whether it would all come together!

By this point, my mind resembled that giant National Lottery tumbler in which numbered balls are bouncing chaotically in every direction! Obviously, the birth was right up there, but I was also constantly thinking of a way that we could successfully finish this walk with everybody unscathed and healthy. Aside from an ageing Jet and the imminent birth of our child, I had agreed with my publisher Pan Macmillan that I would have my first book about the journey handed in this coming August. It was now April, and not a word had been written due to the intensity of the walk around the UK coast – it was all-consuming and gave me no opportunity to sit still and write.

It was dawning on me that I would have to write my first book during the first three months of my newborn baby's life, while Kate recovered from the birth – we had no particular plan for when we were going to restart the walk; it was more a case of waiting for both mother and baby to be ready. This was coupled with the fact that I hadn't really written anything since school, where I had been essentially deemed rubbish at English. I had no experience when it came to writing and, what's more, had never owned a laptop in my life! I knew I would have to handwrite the entire thing the old-fashioned way, with trusty pen and paper, and Kate would then try to make sense of my scrawl and somehow find the time and energy to type it all up while caring for our new baby. *Shit!* I'd often think. *This is going to be fun!* But as the walk so far had shown me, and it's something I will remind myself for the rest of my life, anything is possible if you put your mind to it.

The only option was to make it happen. I would never sit and think, *I just can't do this*. All my thoughts were focused on *how* I could! It's the only way if you want to succeed. I had no choice: it was not just me any more; with a young family soon to be cemented by the birth of a child, I now had a responsibility, and I just couldn't fail, not this time.

18

Plan Bs

Having watched Kate carry our baby month after month along the coastline of England, my admiration and love for her were almost at bursting point. I wanted her in my life for ever. I couldn't spend more than a few intense days around anybody without needing my own space, but with Kate it was different. I had found my soulmate and best friend, and I wanted her to know how much I loved her and to express my commitment to her, as she had to me, Jet and our unborn child. With that in mind, I had made the decision a few months before arriving at our Dorchester retreat to ask her to be my wife.

Knowing Kate, I knew that a million-pound diamond ring wouldn't mean a thing to her. She was all about the effort. And thank God, as I didn't have more than £80 to my name. I got my thinking cap on and realized I knew just the person to help. When I first met Kate at the Whaligoe Steps, I gave her a woollen hat that had been handmade by Kathleen, James's wife from Shetland, both of whom were mentioned in my first book, *Finding Hildasay*. I had used that hat throughout my stay on the uninhabited island, and I knew how much it meant to Kate when I gave it to her. I called Kathleen and asked if it was possible to use her skills and knit an engagement ring in Shetland wool. She loved the idea.

'Chris, I still have with me leftover Shetland wool that I made your hat from!' she added.

'Absolutely perfect!' I said. 'How bloody lovely!'

Kathleen got to work and in no time I received three beautiful Shetland woollen rings, each made in a different colour combination using the same colours as the hat I had given Kate on the very first day that we met. Only a week before the arrival of our baby, Kate had been taken out for the day by a group of local Dorset ladies who were in on the plan. The idea was to take her for an outdoor 'baby shower' on the clifftops in Portland, involving a day of crafts and games, while I stayed back at camp and set up a woodland area for my wedding proposal. I positioned candles all around, set up a steel cooking plate hanging over a fire to cook us a lovely meal, there was a bottle of alcohol-free bubbly, and I set a table decorated with wildflowers all ready to surprise her. It was about 400 yards away from our yurt in a separate woodland where we would spend a night in a beautiful fairy-lit wooden dome called a 'bender tent', so named because it is supported by long bits of wood bent over at the top like a tepee to create more room. I was so nervous it was unbelievable, and I wanted this so much! All she had to do was say YES! My efforts had taken nearly the whole day, and with the little time left before her return, I paced about telling myself that this time tomorrow I could either be engaged to the woman of my dreams, or feeling pretty deflated.

When she returned, she was really tired and slumped down on the bed in the yurt. She said she was pretty much ready to call it a day and go to sleep.

Shit! I thought.

'Kate, why don't we do something a little different and go and stay down in the other woods tonight just to give us a break from being in the yurt all the time? We could get a nice fire on outside and just do something different. It would be lush!' I said, doing my best to persuade her.

'Oh, I really can't be bothered tonight. I'm knackered! It was such a great day, but what can I say? I must've expended all my energy guessing the foods on the various nappy stains! I'm deadbeat. Can we just do it another time? I just want to conk out and get an early night.'

I went outside to gather my thoughts and conjure a plan B. I hoped, knowing Kate and her love for spontaneity, that she would come round. A few minutes later, she emerged from the yurt. 'Come on then,' she said. 'I've managed to peel myself off the bed! Let's go for it. You only live once!'

Thank goodness, I thought to myself, *it's back on.*

With Jet plodding along behind us, we walked down to the woodland where I stopped about 30 yards shy of my efforts, before she could see what I had done. I told her to put her hands over her eyes and I'd guide her as a bit of fun. It was now approaching dusk and the candles had started to take effect. When she opened her eyes, she had a tear in her eye.

'How stunning, and what a lovely thing to do,' she said.

It must've taken me around an hour – rushing around checking none of the meat or vegetables were burning – to finally muster up the courage just before we were about to sit down and eat. 'Darling, come here,' I said, 'give me a cuddle.' We stood nose to nose just looking at each other. This was the moment!

'I'm going to marry you one day, you know that,' I said.

She smiled, and said, 'I hope so!'

It was now or never! I got down on one knee and pulled out one of the woollen rings from a small pouch Kathleen had made in the same tartan material as my kilt. It had a red ribbon around it with a heart in the middle. The woollen ring had a tiny bit of blue sea glass that had been found on the Dorset coast glued to the wool and was acting as my million-pound diamond. I looked up at Kate, who by now I think knew what was happening, as tears started to form around her eyes. 'Marry me, Kate. I love you so much, I want to be with you for the rest of my life!'

I don't think she could believe what was happening – I had certainly taken her by surprise. We'd discussed getting married at some point in the distant future, but *after* the walk; for now, it was parked till more convenient time.

Kate nodded with tears running down her cheeks. 'Yes, I'll marry you!' she said.

You nailed it, mate, I thought to myself, cuddling Kate and giving Jet a wink as if she'd been in on the plan with me the whole time and wanted to congratulate me with a 'Well done, Dad!'

It was a beautiful evening, made even more special knowing that any day now our love for each other would take a physical form in the shape of a child. Just perfect.

It was four in the morning on 30 April when I woke to Kate saying softly, 'Chris, I didn't want to wake you earlier than necessary, but I've been sat up for a couple of hours now and I've got a really intense pain literally every couple of minutes. I've rung the midwives already and they've said the contractions are already frequent enough for someone to come as soon as they're free. I think this is it!'

Oh my God, oh my God started running through my brain like a steam train! It was at this point that I realized how much I wished I was simply putting her in the car and taking her to hospital. There was a lot to do and all I wanted was to sit with Kate. Still half asleep, I jumped out of the bed, grabbed the water pipe and started to unravel it. As I sprinted towards the house along a dark narrow dirt path, I tripped on a tree root and fell right into a bunch of stinging nettles. Disoriented and unable to see, I used the bushes to guide me to the house where the outside light was turned on, giving me much needed visibility!

Hearing the commotion and me trying to get into the

front door to attach the hose to the hot-water tap must have woken Ralph. I realized that something was wrong with the pipe, and in my frustrated commotion, Ralph came running down and we frantically tried everything, but for whatever reason the water was just not coming through. *Shit*, I thought, *bloody typical! This had worked fine twice before and now it decides to do this!*

There was only one option. Ralph grabbed a couple of gorilla tubs (plastic tubs with thin plastic handles usually used for mixing during building work) and we got a system going where I would run down the path into the yurt with a full tub of hot water whilst Ralph stayed at the other end, filling the next one ready for me to collect! When I tipped the first tub in, I could see that this was hardly making a dent. I knew this was going to be a bloody long night, but I didn't expect the birth of a child to be a full-on fitness session! The constant lugging around of huge heavy water bottles that summer had stood me in good stead, however; I hobbled up and down that path with tub after tub of hot water (and they were definitely not light) like a scene from an old slapstick comedy! God, I was knackered, but over the course of a few hours, we managed to get the birthing pool filled, much to Kate's delight!

The midwife finally arrived around 6 a.m. and we waited what felt like an eternity for Kate to dilate enough, but it just wasn't happening. Kate's contractions had been so strong and quick in succession that she had basically been in full-blown active labour from the get-go – there was no build-up! I really felt for her; she'd barely had a break between contractions for hours, but now things seemed to have hit a standstill. I began to realize that giving birth in the yurt in a birthing pool was no longer going to be an option.

The midwives swapped over after a six-hour shift and I think gave it as long as they could in the hope things would progress. Kate was now sixteen hours in, four of which had been spent in the pool, but, by 2 p.m., she had still only dilated a couple of centimetres and the midwife felt there could be potential complications if we continued in the yurt. The call was made that Kate would be taken to Dorchester County Hospital. I knew Kate would be devastated, as she was excited to give birth in the pool in the magic of the yurt, surrounded by nature, as had become the lifestyle she had grown to love. The one thing she'd really tried to focus on throughout the last trimester was preparing for the labour; she'd spent night after night in the tent with her headphones on listening to a hypnobirthing course, all in the hope that she would do everything she could to put her in the right mindset to birth her baby naturally. I knew she'd be gutted. However, she was also pragmatic about it and knew that every birth plan was subject to change, and that the most important thing was for mum and baby to come out of this experience safely. She agreed and got out of the pool to get changed. She was in so much pain, crying and screaming – it was torture to watch!

We phoned Kate's mum, who had been in the area for the past few days visiting, and told her that Kate was in labour. She immediately rushed to the yurt and after a few hours the midwives said we'd have to wait too long for an ambulance, so it was decided that Kate's mum would drive us in the car. By this point, Kate was almost hysterical, screaming in pain every time we went over bumps, which were frequent until we hit the main road. It almost brought me to tears, but I knew that I had to remain calm in the storm to reassure her and even cracked the odd joke, which, as you can imagine, went down like a lead balloon!

During our time at the yurt, we had made friends with the most wonderful lady called Anna Stiles, who had gone above and beyond taking us to the supermarket every week, ensuring we always had shopping, and offered a lift any time we needed to get anywhere. She was adamant that she would be there for us whenever Kate went into labour and had offered to look after Jet while I was in the hospital with Kate. How we would manage a hospital birth with Jet had been a major weight on my mind, and something we knew we needed to organize in advance just in case. Jet obviously wouldn't be allowed inside the hospital, and her separation anxiety when away from me meant that we wouldn't be able to leave her back in the yurt with anybody else. Kate's mum and Anna – both of whom Jet was familiar with – would both take turns looking after Jet in their cars in the hospital car park, and I would run out to see her when I could to help keep her calm.

I had a gut feeling that something was terribly wrong, as I knew Kate and how little fuss she made even in the toughest conditions. About an hour after we arrived, now eighteen brutal hours into labour, it was decided that Kate should have her waters broken to help move things along. She then spent another few hours in a hospital birthing pool. Her contractions now almost seemed non-stop – there was so little break between them that she couldn't even manage to eat a Fruit Pastille! I would try to give her a couple for energy, and she would just spit them out immediately, unable to chew a thing. Then it was out of the pool again and into a hospital bed. No matter what they did, nothing seemed to be happening. I know Kate had wanted to do this without any medical intervention other than painkillers and gas and air, but in the end, she agreed to a half dose of epidural, which would still enable her to feel but hopefully help her to dilate. It was at this point that I took the midwifes outside and said, 'I need you to give Kate something that will ease the pain so she can at least rest.' Once they'd administered the painkiller and it had kicked in, Kate was able to nap for a couple of hours. The feeling of utter helplessness on my part was unbearable; apart from being there for Kate, there was nothing I could do but watch. At around midnight, she had finally dilated 10cm, but after another four hours of pushing, the baby still wasn't making an appearance. The midwives could just about feel the top of the head, but it appeared to be stuck. Try as she might, she just couldn't push the head down any further. This continued with Kate pushing as hard as she could for a good few hours, but I could see she was just exhausted – she was completely done, so much so that no gas or air was making the slightest difference! I was so worried but was still trusting in the midwives and nurses, who obviously knew far more than I did.

Knowing that Kate was going to have to stay in hospital, I nipped down to the car to check on Jet. Kate's mum had gone back to her hotel by now and Anna was doing the night shift in the car park with her. I spoke to Anna about the situation. I was in a mess, and Anna did her best to make me laugh, saying, 'I don't know many men who would run downstairs every hour to check their dog is okay while their woman was in labour!' Somehow, she managed to raise a smile from me.

When I got back, the doctor came in to examine Kate again. She had now been in labour for just under twenty-nine hours! There was discussion of forceps and a ventouse delivery, but the head needed to be further down still for that. The doctor said, 'Let's give it two more hours of pushing, and if nothing happens by then let's get her in for surgery.'

I looked at Kate, who looked at me with the most soul-destroyed look on her face. I know Kate would have kept going for as long as she physically could, but I felt strongly that this baby needed to come out, and it needed to come out now. My patience had shattered. There was no way I was letting Kate suffer for another two hours! I stepped outside, chased the doctor down and in a very stern voice said to her, 'You need to get that baby out now! She can't take any more, and I can see it. You need to take her down to surgery now!' She looked at me, shocked, but she could see I meant what I said. Kate really was done, and her heart rate had slowed. 'I'll go down and assemble a team to prepare for theatre for a Caesarean,' she replied.

It took around an hour, but I felt some comfort in knowing something was happening. When I told Kate, all she said was, 'Thank you, thank you!'

'Kate,' I said, 'I know this is awful for you right now, but just know that in an hour you're going to be cuddling up with your baby and all this will be worth it!'

Her eyes smiled. I could tell by her look that the muscles in her face were unable to muster much more than that!

Soon enough, we were in theatre. When people had told me before that they'd had a baby via Caesarean section, I never really understood the true extent of how strong you have to be to deal with such a thing. As I write this book, I have three molars that need to be yanked from my mouth after an incident I had on a Hebridean island that cracked some teeth. The thought of that alone makes me wince, and I'm forever putting it off, but to say yes to somebody cutting open your abdomen and uterus with a scalpel and pulling a baby out of it is incredibly hardy and brave – I never realized just how much until this moment!

19

Meeting Magnus

I could tell something wasn't quite right. Kate had expelled so much energy over the past thirty hours, all while being completely unable to eat anything except an orange, which was a good twenty hours ago by this point. As she lay on the operating table she was slurring her words, but putting on a brave face, always trying to form a smile and answer the questions the doctors were asking her. She was very pale and clammy-looking. I don't think there had been any point in my life up until now that I had felt so completely and utterly useless. I was a rabbit in a hound's mouth. All I could do was wait and watch.

We didn't know the sex of the baby and wanted it to be a surprise, but I have no shame in admitting that given the fact that my two brothers and I had all had girls so far (five between us in total, which was absolutely great, don't get me wrong), I just liked the idea of having a boy in the family! So I think it would be safe to say that I was wishing for the baby to be a boy.

As I chatted away to Kate, trying to make her excited, suddenly the doctor delivering the baby pulled up a little boy, healthy and covered in pregnancy slime!

'Kate, Kate, it's a little baby boy!' I told her, my voice bursting with excitement, relief and pure surprise.

She looked up to see our baby being pulled up above the blue screen, so that we could see him for the first time. I then cut the umbilical cord and he was passed to Kate, so mother and son could bond skin to skin. Kate was beaming! She finally had her baby in her arms and was a mother for the first time, something I know she had always wanted.

This beautiful moment was suddenly interrupted when, a couple of minutes later, I was rushed to stand behind Kate. I sensed a real sense of urgency among the staff and the doctors present called for another specialist doctor to come down. Something was wrong. Kate was shaking uncontrollably as the doctors and nurses started saying, 'Stay with me, Kate, stay with me!' They handed me our baby, who was now wrapped in a blanket and absolutely beautiful. Although I should've been delighted and jumping for joy, my focus was on Kate.

Anxiety and a high level of distress filled the room as the doctors and nurses swarmed around Kate like bees. I was taken into a separate room with the baby, turning to take one last look at her before I went through the door. She was dropping in and out of consciousness with an incredibly low heart rate and the midwife standing over her head continuously repeating, 'Stay with me, Kate.'

I took a second to look down and take in our new arrival. In that moment I really felt that I would gain a baby boy and lose his mother and my fiancée all in the space of ten minutes. I cried so hard. They were two of the most powerful and conflicting emotions I know I will ever experience. There are no words to describe such a thing – such a loss and such a gain at the same time. A nail-biting ten minutes later, the doctor came in to tell me that it seemed Kate had had an allergic reaction to one of the drugs in the injection she'd been given to stop any blood clotting after the operation. They thought the reaction had probably also been exacerbated by how weak she was, given her lack of food and exhausted state. She didn't have to tell me – I could see by the way Kate looked. That reaction had nearly killed her. Finally, after a torturous half an hour, I was told Kate's heart rate was stable and she had come back around. That's a feeling you don't experience every day! I immediately returned with her son and gave him to her. It had been thirty-one hours in total. Now reunited, with Kate holding her baby boy, it had all been worth it. I already loved the name Magnus – to me, it was such a powerful name and, on the first night of meeting Kate on the Whaligoe Steps, I'd told her the story of Magnus, who I'd met on the island of Foula, and of his ancestral photo album in which every male in every generation of his family line was called Magnus. I can't speak for Kate, but I knew that if I were ever to have a baby boy – which, at the time, was an unlikely prospect – I'd want to call him

Magnus. Luckily for me, Kate shared the same love for the name.

Magnus Edward Arden Lewis. Born at 5.35 a.m. on 1 May 2022

There's no telling just how a woman's body is going to react after giving birth, and for Kate, unfortunately, she was one of the unlucky ones. It really took its toll on her and even to this day, she is still recovering. But what was most important was that she had given birth to the most beautiful baby boy. It was so clear to see that she was a natural mother from the second she took him in her arms. A mother's love is truly something magical to behold.

It was a real excitement for us to know we were giving Magnus the very best start to life he could possibly ask for, even if our life was a little unconventional. To most people in this country, the idea of having a baby out in cold temperatures is simply out of the question, but we knew better. For as long as humans have existed prior to the past 150 years, let's say, babies have been raised and brought up outside with only fires to keep warm – no central heating or any of the excessive modern-day luxuries we are now conditioned by mass marketing to believe they need today. In fact, if you go to Iceland, you'll see it's normal for babies to be wrapped up tight in woolly rugs and left outside the back door in their prams in the cold, because their parents know it's good for their immune system. Humans thrived in the cold, becoming the most dominant species on this planet!

That aside, Kate and I knew that all a baby really needs is unconditional love and nurture from mum and dad, and the basics like food and milk! With this, we were excited to get back out there on the walk and introduce Magnus to the outside world, living in a way that was so different from the norm. But first we needed to conjure a plan to make this work!

After a month or so of Kate trying everything in her power, it also turned out that she seemed to be suffering from every unfortunate issue under the sun when it came to breastfeeding. She would do her best to pump for as long as possible, but Magnus would have to be bottle-fed, which meant carrying a lot more in the way of equipment.

The more time went by, the clearer it became that there was simply no way that Kate and I would be able to carry everything that was needed for Magnus, and everything required for Jet, coupled with the reality that Kate was now in for a much longer recovery post-surgery. We would be on the move daily, which meant transporting *everything* we needed with us.

There were also the restrictions down south to take into account; wild camping was illegal, as was making fires, which we would inevitably need for warmth given the fact that we would soon be heading into winter. It was time to get my 'A Team' head on and work out a solution!

Nothing was going to stop us from finishing this walk – not difficult logistics, not landowners, and certainly not the restrictive camping laws that took away our access to the outdoors. It's really quite unbelievable when you think that less than 10 per cent of England is accessible to the public. It's a beautiful country, of that there is absolutely no doubt, but money and greed have swept over this land like a plague. Someone somewhere was making money from the freedom that should be available to all without question – the freedom of simply being outside! I thought about those that can't afford to pay for this access; car parks and National Trust entry rates for instance; those who probably need to be out and about more than anyone, and it made my blood boil. I really couldn't get the idea out of my head that opportunities for making money seemed to far outweigh the health of the nation.

Often, at night-time, while in the yurt, I would think a lot about having had a taste of proper freedom over my three and a half years walking in Scotland. Down in England, even if we think we are, we are not free. I completely understand that society needs to be governed and requires a system for things to work, otherwise the world would end up resembling *Mad Max*, but as the years go by more and more of our basic human rights seem to be getting stripped away from us. Kate and I were by now more and more determined to get out of the societal rat race, in which the rich only seem to get richer and the poor get poorer, and a government supposedly working in our best interests is making decisions that, in my mind, only serve to make us worse off. The government's agenda is clearly a world away from really taking care of nature and supporting the nation to live healthier, happier lives by getting outside. Take the recent controversy with Exmoor National Park for example, when the landowner initially won the right to deny a generations-old pastime of people camping under the stars there (now thankfully revoked, I understand, after much public uproar), and the more recent decision to approve the use of a huge oil field out in the North Sea.

I'd made up my mind a long time ago that I really would rather live in a cave away from it all than be subjected to the treadmill of modern-day life. As I grow older and hopefully wiser, with a better understanding of the world around me, I often wonder what kind of world our little Magnus is being brought into. Quite frankly, it's scary. I would sit in that yurt and ask myself: *In a hundred years' time, when my grandchildren are having their children, where on earth will we be as a race?*

It's amazing how breaking away from it all can make you look at it from a different perspective. I'd been starting to realize how totally mental it had all become since my first lockdown, where I was busy surviving on the island of Hildasay while the rest of the nation was going crazy over toilet roll. Witnessing these events, I made up my mind that I would do everything in my power to make sure these generations know and understand how to live in the great outdoors, as at some point in the future, who knows when, it wouldn't surprise me if that's exactly where the human race ends up – returning to our roots, having realized we cannot undo what we've done to this earth unless something changes very quickly.

One night in the yurt, after playing the guitar to Magnus as he lay in bed only two days after he was born, it suddenly hit me that I needed to get to work writing. I first put my pen to paper three days after he was born, and very quickly realized that, as expected, this was not going to be easy! Incredibly early mornings, helplessly watching the excruciating trauma of Kate and Magnus's breastfeeding experience, and endless sleepless nights meant squeezing in the time to write in any spare second I could find. We were now completely out of money as well, so when we finally received a small payment from the publisher, it was a huge relief.

I sat down with Kate and said, 'How I'm going to get this book written? I just don't know, but I'll do it. I promise you, I have never in my life missed a deadline, and this won't be the first.' I meant it, and I knew she believed I could do it.

'I have a plan, darling,' I said to Kate. 'With the money that we've just been paid, we need to buy a van. We need to be completely self-sufficient going back on this walk. There's no way in this world that, if something were to go wrong with Magnus and we needed to get him to hospital in the middle of the night, or even if something was wrong with you given your complications, we could just rely on the general public to help us out. It's not their responsibility, it's mine, and I won't be able to sleep at night knowing that this kind of thing could happen and we aren't able to rely on ourselves to get it sorted.'

'I'm with that,' Kate agreed. 'We can't rely on the kindness of followers and certainly can't be in a position where we need to ring strangers in the middle of the night and expect them to answer, let alone come to our aid. We need to do what's right by Magnus and that absolutely means being able to rely on ourselves.'

With that agreed, I bought a bare white Vauxhall van from a mechanic in Dorset for £3,600. At the end of

June, we would have to leave Moignes Court and say goodbye to Ralph and his wife, Dizzy, to find another place to stay, as Kate was not ready to get back on the walk just yet, and I still needed time to finish my book. Once I'd bought the van, I got to work on it immediately and, between writing the book, being a new dad and all the chores that come with that, I'd spend every hour possible getting out and transforming the back of a work van into a temporary motorhome!

What I didn't know was that the man who'd sold us this van had completely screwed us over! I'm ashamed to admit that, although I know the very basics, I am not much of a mechanic. I'd just finished building a makeshift single bed in the back from whatever scraps of timber I could find lying around Moignes Court, and needed to head out to the local Co-op to get some food supplies, when about a minute after I'd turned out of the driveway, the engine exploded and smoke and steam started to fill the van.

I jumped out to let Jet out the back and watched as our only hope to finish the walk went up in smoke in front of my eyes. I was soul-destroyed, although I will say I did have a little chuckle to myself at just how devastatingly comical and typically unlucky this entire situation was! Sometimes all you can do is laugh at adversity, so it loses its sting. And it could have been much worse – I could have had Magnus and Kate with me. And thank God, it didn't happen in the middle of nowhere.

But I really wasn't looking forward to telling Kate that the van I'd assured her was going to get us around the rest of England was now sitting 400 yards up the road in smoke, not to mention my so-called 'reliable' investment with nearly all of our money! But hey, what can you do? Just another bump in the road and a hurdle to cross.

On hearing what had happened, Anna Stiles, who by this point had become another lifelong friend, lent us the money to get a second-hand engine to save the van without a single hesitation. It was an absolute lifeline, and as much as it killed us to have to owe anybody money, it was our only choice. We accepted Anna's generosity knowing once I'd delivered the book and got paid by Pan Macmillan, we could pay back our dear friend in full.

With the van up and running again and Magnus now two months old and a bundle of smiling joy, we said goodbye to Ralph, Dizzy, their boys and the community of Moignes Court and left for Kate's mum's back in Malvern.

After another month of solid writing, most of which I'd spent in Kate's dad's empty flat while she stayed at her mum's looking after Magnus, on 29 July, a day before my deadline, I somehow managed to complete my book, *Finding Hildasay*. It had been an incredibly hot summer, at times reaching 40 degrees, and I can assure you, sitting cooped up in a bedroom sweating my nuts off writing a book was not how I'd envisaged the authorial process. I'd always romantically said that I would retreat to a bothy somewhere in Scotland to write my first book, and this was a world away from that. But the main thing was, it was done!

The sense of sheer relief and pressure off my shoulders,

knowing that now I could plough my energy back into the walk and of course my family, was unbelievable! I actually think I had a little tear of joy. I rang Kate. 'I'm coming home, darling – I did it! Let's get back out there and get this walk in the bag, shall we?'

We were both so excited to get back to the outdoor life. Kate carefully and efficiently packed all the gear that we needed for Magnus, and I sorted the van out. It had no rear windows or amenities, with just a timber frame for a single bed, so Kate could have a mattress with Magnus to help make her more comfortable given her C-section. It was laughable really – and we did laugh! But it was all part of the adventure. 'Let's do this!' we said.

We said our goodbyes to Kate's mum, thanked her for all she had done, and as we drove away, I saw a little tear in Liz's eye. Excited and raring to get a three-month-old baby out there, we headed for Hastings, where we had left off. With Magnus strapped into his car seat, we drove off unaware that disaster was about to strike once again!

Only fifteen minutes into our journey and around 200 yards from joining the M5, which would take us down south, out of the blue, the van suddenly died a death! All the warning lights came on and she just stopped. Thankfully, we hadn't yet pulled onto the motorway and there was a layby into which I was able to steer the van. I tried the ignition a few times, but nothing.

Kate and I looked at each other solemnly and burst out laughing. We rang the AA and it soon became clear that we wouldn't be going anywhere that day. We needed to get Magnus off the roadside and somewhere safe.

'You're going to have to phone your mum, Kate!' I said.

I am pretty sure the poor woman was looking forward to a bit of alone time after putting us up for a month, but no such luck! With that, just forty minutes after heading off, Liz came to collect Kate and Magnus to get them off the road and back home, while I stayed with the van.

We got the van towed back to Liz's house, but when the mechanic came to look at it, the verdict was bleak. 'Chris, pal,' he said, 'I hate to be the breaker of bad news, but this is scrap! It will cost you more to get this sorted than it would to buy a new one!'

As he spoke, I was already working on a new alternative, and there was only one man that sprung to mind that might help – our loyal and good friend Steve. To give you an idea of what this guy is like, the second I called him to ask for any advice or even what I could do, he stopped me and came up with a plan there and then. He dropped everything, got into the blue Volkswagen transporter T4 that he had used to pick us up for our first scans pre-Magnus, and headed down from Birmingham to Malvern. 'Chris, mate, do you know how much I just want to help? That time we drove north to Scotland and Skye, do you have any idea how much you helped me? I was broke. Take the van, pal. Use it for as long as you like. I need to get back to work now,' and just like that, he was gone and on a train back to Birmingham!

I couldn't believe it; his gesture was incredibly kind, and the van itself was a massive upgrade to the piece of shit I'd purchased from that deceitful seller. It had carpeted walls, back seats that folded down into a bed, and rear windows. It was a damn sight better than the tin can we had been about to set off in! Steve's kindness really made me emotional and hit a spot. *God*, I thought to myself, *imagine if we all just helped each other like this – what a wonderful place we would live in!*

As hard as it was in the first three years of my walk, at least I'd enjoyed it and got a real sense of satisfaction each night, sleeping under the stars, rewarding myself with cosy fires, breath-taking scenery and beautiful people. Don't get me wrong – we had met some incredible people in England too – but recently, I'd been bottled on the head and now ripped off with the van, and I felt like a child in school constantly getting told off for putting up a tent! To me, England was like living with a pair of super-strict parents who would never let you do anything. I felt sad that I was craving the end of the walk, rather than gutted that I was finishing. It's not how I'd envisioned drawing this adventure to a close, at all, but it's how it was and I just had to suck it up and get on with it.

The book was done, our baby son was healthy and strong, Kate was on the mend and Jet was still with us, so huge obstacles had been crossed. And now, we had a new lease of life with the van! 'Focus on the positives, Chris, that's how winning is done!'

I unloaded all our gear from the broken-down van and transferred it into the T4 immediately. The next morning, we made our second attempt at getting down to Hastings.

20

Freedom!

The T4 van did the trick and we arrived back in Hastings within three and a half hours. I could sense a change in myself, an almost fresh approach to the walk. As grateful as I was to have been put up for three months in the yurt and at Kate's mum's, it made me feel confined at times. I'd spent too long living under the stars. By now, I was a living manifestation of the phrase 'some birds are just not supposed to be caged'. Although, in my view, I believe this goes for us all deep down. I knew that we would have a lot to learn about the logistics of the walk now that we had a baby in tow, but we would learn it on the go and, if anything, the fact that I'd been cooped up in the house writing for so long, plus the weeks inside after Jet's operation, just being in the outdoors again felt amazing! I think all of us including Jet were happy to once again be cooking meals in the fresh air, walking each day and taking in the scenery.

From the gentrified Georgian houses and smart pier at Hastings, we made our way east along the south coast through the rest of East Sussex and Hampshire to Portsmouth. From there we would head over to the Isle of Wight.

It was incredibly rewarding to experience nature along the coast with Magnus each day and seeing his first-time awe and curiosity awaken. Watching his delight at waves lapping at the shore or him laughing under trees as he saw their leaves swaying in the breeze was simply magical. The buzz of having a van and being fresh back on the walk was very novel. Initially, we spent a few days sleeping in the van in Hastings National Park car park. It was still August and the height of tourist season, so the four of us trying to camp surreptitiously proved too much of a ball-ache – we'd have to walk miles from the van with all our gear to find a spot sufficiently hidden away, but it wasn't too difficult to find little car parks we could sneak into for the night to get to sleep. Campsites were not our style, but with very limited options and still wanting to use the tent as much as possible, we used them a fair bit. This was all good and well, but most at this time a year were costing us around £40 a night and were packed; we may as well have had holes in our pockets, and there was so much noise at night-time, it was far from ideal for a three-month-old baby who needed lots of sleep.

It soon became apparent that a 28-kilo dog, a fully grown woman, a fully grown man and a baby in the back of a small 2001 VW T4 was going to be a very tough gig, a scenario that, in any other situation, we would only want to put up with for a few nights, maximum! Looking back, we were walking each day, living outside without amenities like a sink and a hob, and Magnus wasn't sleeping through the night. To be this squashed every night meant we struggled to achieve even the bare minimum of sleep! Jet, having been so close to me since I'd adopted her, was adamant she was getting her share of the bed, and believe me when I say there's no stopping a hound who demands space!

Magnus had a small, cocoon-type nest bed with raised cushioned edges all around to stop him from falling out and us from rolling onto him, but that alone was the width of a fully grown adult! Knowing how uncomfortable this was for both me and Kate, with such a small slither of space either side of Magnus's bed, and aware that Kate was in need of more space than I was, given that she'd had a Caesarean only a few months before, I would spend my nights lying with my feet tucked up in the foetal position, with Jet nestled at the bottom of the bed where I slept. I can honestly say that sleeping without a roll mat in winter in Shetland was more comfortable than this! I barely slept at all. But what could I do? Occasionally, if we found a car park quiet enough next to a woodland, I would pitch up and sleep in the tent next to the van in the hope that at least one of us could get a slightly better kip! We persisted and persisted but there were times when we felt like we had reached the end of our tethers with the sleeping arrangements. This lasted from August through to the end of the walk.

One of the biggest logistical challenges for us was having to sterilize Magnus's bottles. In my view, I'm not sure if everything we're told we need on this front is 100 per cent necessary or just yet another product that is sold to us making us *think* we need it. I'd often say to Kate, 'How the hell did our ancestors do it?' Magnus needed about eight feeds a day and we needed to have all the bottles prepped for the day in advance. Kate was still insistent on doing her best to breastfeed by using two portable, USB-rechargeable breast pumps that she would wear while walking and in the van at night. I could tell this wasn't going to last, as it was just proving too much of a headache to clean them as regularly and efficiently as needed, but I was not going to argue with a woman who has just given birth! We had a lot to wash and sterilize.

Our daily routine included boiling enough water in our cooking pot on the gas stove to pour into a foldable plastic bucket in which to wash eight bottles. We would then sterilize them in more boiling water. I would then have to boil another litre or so to fill them all. The boiling water would then cool inside the bottles and be ready to add formula for use, seeing us through all of Magnus's night feeds and the following morning. Whenever she could, Kate would fill these with pumped breast milk, but her supply had never been enough to provide all the milk he needed this way and so he had been partly formula-fed from early days. It became clear that continuing to pump was becoming too difficult to keep up and by the time we hit mid-September, Kate had to come to terms with the end of her breastfeeding journey. From now on, we switched to using formula full-time. This meant needing more water and the added expense of buying formula twice a week; it was time-consuming, but these things can never be helped. This was what we needed to do, and we simply got on with it.

As we headed into winter now nearing Brighton, our nightly routine after a day's walking was quite relentless! Finding a car park would sometimes take hours once we started heading through more built-up areas along the coast such as Brighton, and we would then get to work sorting out the next twelve hours' worth of bottles for Magnus before finally cooking our dinner. Wind, rain, hail, snow – no matter what happened, we still had to cook food and we still had to sterilize Magnus's bottles every night.

I found that after months of struggling to find decent enough spots to park the van each night, my excitement at being back on the walk soon dulled. Being in the van at night started to feel like being shut in a suitcase to sleep. As the nights got colder, I would just sit outside and wish we had a nice cosy fire to warm the bones before bed, but instead we would all nestle in the back of the van like sardines and just hope that one of us would get some kip! The same process with the bottles and breakfast would be repeated first thing every morning when I set my alarm and got up before anybody woke. It was a lot of work, but I always looked forward to those little moments outside where I could just sit on my own and go through my head how the next day was going to work.

The dynamic of the walk had obviously completely changed. It was amazing to do it with our boy, but each day took a lot of logistical thought and planning.

I think people on social media thought the reason we were going so slow was because we had a baby, but this really wasn't the case – it was actually Jet that dictated the pace at which we would move forward daily. As time went on, it was becoming more evident that Jet was starting to slow down considerably. It was about to make the walk a whole lot tougher, but out of respect and loyalty to her, which she had always paid us, it was a given that the whole walk would now work around her.

Once we got going again at Hastings, we decided that the rest of this walk would have to be done separately, with Jet taking time out in the van to preserve her strength. The main issue to overcome with this plan was Jet's anxiety when I wasn't around her. To combat that, our best option was to drive to our starting point and for me to run rather than walk, or at least move as fast as my legs could carry me to get back to Jet quicker, while Kate stayed in or around the van with Magnus to look after her. I would choose a spot around 4 or 5 miles down the coast where Kate could drive the van to meet me. We would then drive back to where I had started my run so that Kate could cover the same section, adamant that she would carry Magnus as she went! It would take much longer for Kate to walk with a baby than it would for me to run as fast as I could, especially given that she would often have to stop for feeds or nappy changes. Sometimes I would do my stretch first or we might do it the other way round, depending on the weather mainly. As with everything, we had to be flexible and work around what was thrown our way each day.

I know some people will read this and think we were crazy, but Kate had walked all this way from Inverness. She had walked and lived outside through two winters and throughout the whole of her pregnancy. She was as determined as I was to carry on walking to the end and keep on living this adventure to the max, rather than stepping aside to become a support driver. I totally understood where she was coming from and this journey had never been about racing to the finish; it was a way of life, and I could see she needed the natural outdoors she so loved, having gone through such a hard time postpartum. When it came to carrying Magnus, I also got it – she was his mother and she wanted to be with him all the time, and for him to experience this outdoor life too.

All of this meant that between us we might only clock up around 10 miles, which meant only five in total from start to finish each day! But the system worked well, and to be honest with you, I was quite glad to be running rather than walking, as the amount of walking while carrying all my possessions for so many years had really taken its toll. It was great to get a different form of exercise and stretch out all the tight muscles for a change. We knew that this was not a race, and the main thing was that we both got round it feeling good in ourselves. Checking the maps, I would sometimes sit in disbelief and think that this could take us another year before we would finish!

What concerned me was how expensive the south coast

was, and how much it was eating through our funds. We had neither fridge nor freezer in the van, which meant we couldn't store food and always had to buy fresh. Kate still had a lot of unfortunate side effects as part of her recovery, and we were very conscious of the importance of eating healthily, which also proved expensive, as did fuel for the van! It really worried me, up to a point where, at times, I thought about mentioning to Kate that maybe she should just stop and let me get on with it to get this nailed and in the bag, but I couldn't bear the thought of not being around little Magnus, or Kate for that matter, and I knew it would've destroyed Kate not to finish what she'd worked so hard for over the past two years, so I just had to accept that we would find a way.

It turned out the instalments from my publisher that I had hoped would be a much-needed nest egg for me and my family when we finished the walk would all be spent on getting us around the rest of it! I'd worked so hard over the past five years to raise money for SSAFA, and I'd never intended to get anything out of it at the end, but things had changed given that I now had a young family to support. It soon became apparent that we would be arriving back in Swansea with nothing to live off. This money was so important to us and I knew that for as long as we were covering only 5 or so miles a day, given our day-to-day costs, it wasn't going to last us to the end.

I remember receiving messages from some people on my social media page, 'Chris Walks the UK', saying that they would buy my book providing all royalties went to SSAFA. I remember thinking to myself, *You cheeky gits,*

if five years of graft raising money for charity isn't enough
for you, especially given the fact that I now have a young
family, I'm not sure what else I'm physically able to give!

Ironically, everything that I was getting from the book
was being put towards us getting around allowing us to
continue to raise money for SSAFA, so essentially, it was
going to them anyway! The fact of the matter is that we
were spending far more than the amount of money being
donated at this point, which was next to nothing. We
thought that donations would really pick up as people
saw how much effort we were putting in doing this with
a baby now, but they barely went up at all. It really hurt
if truth be told, as we were working harder than ever from
the second our eyes opened to the second we fell asleep.
To me it felt like work, work, work without a single
moment of rest, and I was unable to take my mind off it
all for a single minute.

By the time we hit the Isle of Wight in October, I
received news that the TV series *New Lives in the Wild,*
presented by Ben Fogle, wanted to do an episode on our
adventure. We were delighted not for the fact that we
were going to be on TV, but because after our last documentary aired, we received around £30,000 in donations
for SSAFA. Given that Ben is so popular and his shows
are always so informative and well presented, I knew this
would probably be our last chance to bump up the donations. We were still sitting at around £260,000, and this
felt like our last big hope if we were to even have a chance
of hitting the £500,000 mark. It was a little ray of hope
and was just the boost to morale that I needed.

21

Ben

On the Isle of Wight, where we stayed for about three weeks, we had the pleasure of spending our whole stay with the most amazing couple who owned a budding vodka company called Tipsy Wight. It was now October and I slept solo in the van in their driveway while Kate and Magnus took a spare bedroom. We'd been so cramped in the van up until this point and the time-hungry routine of sterilizing and boiling water could now be condensed to ten minutes thanks to running water and the use of a kettle. Our hosts were so welcoming, and every night after a long day's walking we'd return to delicious home-cooked meals, playing the guitar and enjoying their brilliant company. The scenery on the Isle of Wight was stunning, with spectacular cliff-top views, gorgeous beaches, the pristine Tennyson Down and the iconic view of the Needles – three stacks of white chalk that stuck out to sea with a red-and-white striped lighthouse. Incredibly, these chalk stacks protruded from a stretch of chalk under the sea that still ran all the way from here to Old Harry Rocks by Studland Bay on the Dorset coast.

We were blessed with some great weather on the Isle of Wight, but once we returned to the mainland, we were now fully into the throes of autumn. As we progressed along the estuary up and around Southampton and then along the rest of the Hampshire coast past Lymington, the nights certainly became colder. By early November, we had made it into Dorset with its stunningly pretty rolling landscapes and Jurassic coastline. We continued through to Bournemouth and walked the entirety of Poole Harbour, which in total I believe is around 50 miles, making it the second largest harbour in the world after Sydney.

With around a week to go now before filming, we paused the walk, staying in and around the Studland area to get prepared for an intense week ahead. I'd spent a good few days pottering around finding good spots for us to film, going so far as taking water and firewood to certain spots where a kind landowner had agreed that it was okay to make a fire on his patch for one of the nights' shooting. Having been able to seek all the necessary landowner permissions, we were able to wild camp for the week, which, even though it was December, got us bubbling with excitement again, and I have to say it was really nice to spend some in-depth time with Ben. The filming took five full days, and we felt excited to share a deeper insight into the reality of life on the walk, particularly now we were hitting winter with a baby. So far, we'd been lucky with all the TV shows we'd worked on, in that all the people that we'd worked with had been great, and that was exactly the case for *New Lives in the Wild*; the whole crew were so friendly, fun and understanding given that we had to be flexible due to Magnus.

Now and then, between filming, we would sit and chat with Ben, sharing tales of adventures and delving into our shared love of Scotland. Ben was so kind, offering advice when I talked about future endeavours and, of course, fielding my questions about the publishing world since he'd so kindly written the foreword for my book. He's such a lovely bloke and was great with Magnus. During our lunch breaks, he'd often sit with him on his lap, giving us a chance to eat, as did some of the film crew! It was a really wonderful experience. When the show finally aired, we were delighted, and it had such amazing feedback, with a lot of Ben's avid followers saying it was the best episode yet! I was so happy that it had come across well. It was a complete success and a welcome break from the seriousness of constantly finding a place to stay in the van.

Once the show aired, my predictions were proven right, and our fundraising jumped up another £40,000 in the space of a few weeks! It was just what we needed, and I can't tell you how happy Kate and I were. To this day, I'm not sure exactly why, but Ben seemed to have a real soft spot for us. I was so incredibly touched by what he said about us at the end of the show, which even brought a tear to his eye. I can hands down tell you now that what you see on television is how Ben is, and it's been a real pleasure to have formed a friendship with this man.

Once filming was over, we resumed the walk up until a few days before Christmas, where we had been given a lovely holiday home near Salcombe on the Devon coast. We were so grateful to have this place as it meant we didn't have to spend our nights searching for spots to park up and sleep in. We instead spent time getting warm and cosy as a family, enjoying the festive spirit and taking our mind off the walk for a few restorative days. After that, we were ready to head to the Channel Islands at the start of the New Year. The Channel Islands were completely different to any other UK islands I'd walked, more for their distant location and history than anything! They were far closer to France than mainland England; Alderney, the most northerly located, was only 8 miles from the Continent. Our time here would see us walk Guernsey first, followed by Herm, Jersey, Sark and Alderney, and it rained constantly for the duration. Both Kate and I were amazed at the abundance of history along the coast on these islands, and we were particularly interested to learn of how the Nazis were left stranded there before the end of the Second World War. The coastlines here were littered with bunkers, gun batteries and huge concrete watch-towers.

As ever, our initial itinerary changed time and time again as we were completely subject to boat crossing changes, given the unpredictable weather. It was now early January and winter had firmly set in. Ironically, it was warmer inside our tent than inside the van (which we had no way of heating), but again, we were informed that wild camping was a no-go here. With no chance of a fire at night, we had little choice but to keep the van running to get some kind of heat in there to settle for the night. It was killing the engine and our fuel that at this point was as sacred to us as water, but there was nothing else for it given the temperature.

For the first week or so on Guernsey, we spent every night sleeping inside the van in a hotel car park that had now shut for the winter. We then had a stroke of luck when a lady called Hannah found out about us from a news item that went out soon after our arrival; she invited us to stay in the shed in her back garden for the duration of our time on the island. They had two young children themselves and were just the most chilled-out, welcoming, friendly family we could have asked to stay with. Hannah, Steve, Hattie and Teddy really made our stay here so special, and we'd once again be leaving having made friends for life.

The two main islands, Guernsey and Jersey, both had some steep sections on certain sides, which made for some very pleasant surprises, as the coast paths wound their way past some seriously picturesque bays, which at this time of year were completely empty. It didn't take long before we sensed a certain rivalry between the two islands, having been told on numerous occasions that this was the case; each person was adamant that theirs was better – that's humans for you!

The smaller islands of Herm and Sark were absolutely

stunning when it came to scenery, but for me, the most exciting part of our adventure on the Channel Islands was my journey to Alderney, the closest to France. We were having major trouble getting here due to the weather. Since the day we arrived, it had absolutely bucketed down with rain, along with the odd angry hailstorm thrown in for good measure. This meant a lot of boat cancellations, and we only had two days left before our return ferry to the mainland was booked (which had already been cancelled and rearranged several times due to the weather conditions). Instead of going the conventional way to get to this island, a local got in touch to offer a small rib that would take around an hour to get over. Given the weather and the fact that it was set to be a very bumpy ride, it was decided it wouldn't be safe enough for Magnus. It turned out that somebody had been in touch with the small Alderney airline as a backup plan, who offered Kate and Magnus free return passage on the small flight over, which would take about twenty minutes.

As I clambered onto the small red boat for the crossing, I felt a rush of excitement. It really took me back to some of my adventures in Scotland, and some of the uninhabited and inhabited islands where we would often take the more adventurous way. I remember being on the back of the boat, thinking to myself, *This is more like it!* The journey over took longer than an hour and it was pretty hair-raising to say the least! Kate and Magnus had already arrived by the time I got off the boat and we pushed hard to get round the island before having to head back. The boat ride back was far less bumpy and as the sun started to set, I noticed, to our left, a pod of dolphins! We stopped the boat and turned off the engines while we watched them splash around so elegantly. It was such a wonderful and lovely moment and, in my mind, a little hello from mother nature, that feeling you are witnessing something so special. It was moments like these back up north in Scotland that had been so plentiful, that had helped me to steer away from my depression when I first started out on my odyssey. It was a fitting end to our time on these special islands.

22

'Chris Runs the Rest of the UK!'

After we returned from the Channel Islands, we walked through Weymouth, where we received an incredible breakfast reception at the local veterans' hub near Portland. We also faced the brutally challenging 18-mile shingle Chesil Beach, which I ended up running. My feet would get stuck in the deep pebbles along this stretch and every step would feel like I was using three times the energy as I would for a normal one.

I'd never been to Devon or any of the south west, but I'd heard some really good things about what was in store for us in these parts. I was so looking forward to it, as was Kate, and neither of us was disappointed. It was now late January, and despite some challenging weather conditions, whenever we had those crisp, bright winter skies or low sun peeping through atmospheric clouds, some of the sights along the coast were really something. It was in these moments that I would forget how hectic, demanding and logistically challenging this walk had become. I relished just looking out to sea and reminding myself of the things I loved about the walk, taking the time to stop whenever nature put on a show for us.

As we started heading further west, the little car parks we had been using to sleep in started getting fewer and further between, and many had height barriers the van wouldn't fit under. Occasionally we'd end up parked overnight on the side of the road, but generally, we had to swallow phenomenally expensive car parking charges that were starting to cripple us financially.

By mid-February, we had reached Dawlish and, only a few days before, Kate had started to feel a nasty niggle in her Achilles heel. This was a real disaster! When about to have a baby, a woman's body goes through a lot of changes, one being that the hormones relax tendons and ligaments, meaning parts of the body loosen for birth. At the time, we had no idea that Kate should have been doing a lot more to help heal and strengthen after her surgery. She had been given the go-ahead to start walking again before we set off and was advised to ease herself back in, which we felt we had been doing with the much lower mileage. However, it seemed that walking from Hastings all the way to Dawlish – including all the islands we'd done, which in places had some very steep terrain – while carrying Magnus had created issues with her Achilles tendons, to the point where she was now badly limping. There was nothing else for it – she would have to stop walking, at least for the time being.

God, she was crushed. As was I. Not only was it a bitter pill to swallow mentally; it also left us with what felt like an almost insurmountable logistical challenge. *What on earth are we going to do?* I kept thinking. *How will we finish this walk?* Jet couldn't walk far these days, and now Kate was unable to walk and struggling even to be active on her feet looking after Magnus, who was now very confidently crawling and always on the move. A couple of days after the diagnosis, I took myself off in the van so I could have a serious think.

This is my fault, I kept telling myself. *It was too much too soon, and I shouldn't have let Kate carry Magnus, no matter how adamant she was that she wanted to. How on earth am I going to get a baby, Jet and a now injured Kate hundreds of miles back to Swansea?* It would've been very easy for us to have quit at this point, it really would. But we'd come so far, and it just wasn't an option. So, while I sat in the van, I had to really contemplate how we were going to make this work. Some people would tell us it was time for Kate to take Magnus back to her mum's and stay there until I finished the walk, but I knew that there was no chance in this world that I was going to leave my son and my fiancée for that long, or to finish this walk alone. We had to find a way to do it together or we didn't do it at all. It really was that simple.

Family is the most important and precious thing that we can have. It is such a gift, and in my mind, no charity walk – or anything for that matter – would take precedence over this. One evening I sat down with Kate, who I could see was completely soul-destroyed. What a monumental effort this woman had put in from the very first day she'd started: she'd given up everything she had worked so hard for in her career, becoming highly respected in the teaching world, to join a charity walk that threw her straight into a Scottish winter and a freezing lockdown; she'd walked the east coast of Scotland, the east coast of England, thirty-seven weeks of which she was pregnant and still living in a tent each night; she'd had a baby on the way round and conquered most of the south coast carrying her newborn while battling a very challenging postpartum experience – and it had all suddenly come to a crashing end because of an ankle injury. I would often joke that she was the Jonny Wilkinson of walkers!

Harsh as it sounds, at the end of the day it was me that started it and it was me that had to finish it. So long as I had walked it all, then the mission to walk the entire UK coastline had still been accomplished. As I told Kate this, she burst into tears. The one way that we could continue this as a unit was for Kate to stop walking and take on a support role; Kate would look after Magnus while I walked, and rest as much as she could in the hope that after a few months she would heal and perhaps even return to walking if her ankle had recovered. In the meantime, I would do the walking and get us round the coast. The other problem would be how I would get plenty of miles in with a dog unable to walk who simply wouldn't stay with anyone else without scratching the door down, tearing the car seats, or escaping through a window.

We resumed the walk where we left off in Dawlish in Devon. We started with Kate dropping me off, playing with Magnus nearby or in the van so she could watch over Jet while I was running my stretch, then picking me up again once I was done. It was a constant worry to me knowing that, although she wasn't walking, Kate had to be so active, and her injury wasn't getting the rest it needed, and if anything this was making it worse. It was a constant fight in my mind between prioritizing the walk and doing what needed to be done for my family. I knew that the sooner I could get this walk finished, the sooner I could take a more active role with Magnus and give Kate the rest she needed.

Once we got going like this though, it became clear that Kate's Achilles injury needed more rest. The only thing we could think of was that she would go back to her mum's with Magnus for a week or two while I got some miles under my belt, moving as fast as I could down the coast to get us that bit closer to home. For now, I was going to have to do this alone, and I would have to have Jet with me, park the van at my starting point with her inside, run a few miles and then go the same distance back on myself to link up with the van again, then drive it down to where I'd got to and keep going slowly but surely this way until I had tired myself out for the day.

There were some occasions when a follower offered to wait with Jet in their car and then come and meet me when I was done with her to take us both back to the van and so on for the morning or afternoon, but as hugely grateful as I was, I felt slightly uncomfortable doing it – not only was it a huge ask for someone, but I also knew Jet felt unnerved waiting with a complete stranger. So, for the most part, I just ran double the distance, going back on myself every few miles. Running the miles in the one direction would have been plenty, but to run it all twice, half of which would be in the wrong direction, was tough-going. I felt like Forrest Gump! However, there was something crazily gratifying about getting it done the hardest way I could imagine; I must be a masochist! There were even times when I went into super drive and would just run and run until I dropped, often banging out more than a marathon a day to utilize the time and get us closer to that finish line and make the most of being on my own with Jet, who was always anxiously awaiting my return. As soon as I arrived back at the van, I would let Jet out and drink a lot of water!

It was now no longer 'Chris Walks the UK', but 'Chris Runs the Rest of the UK Twice'! I would always sleep in the van in the evening and get up at first light, drive to the next section of coast and plot out car parks along the next stretch.

There is no doubt that I was getting fitter, but towards the end of the day, especially if I'd put in a lot of miles, psychologically it was crushing. If I continued like this from Dawlish, South Devon, and up to Swansea, I worked out it was the same distance as running from Newcastle to London! As I made my way further through Devon, the coastline itself was really lovely. I was so pleased that the change in the walk had happened here, and I didn't have to find myself sprinting through major built-up areas by big towns and cities. Instead, it was lovely scenic areas with rolling green hills and high sea cliffs pretty much all the way down to Penzance. I was losing a lot of weight now due to the nature of the running, and I could see it in my face, which was getting a lot thinner.

Running is so different to walking, and to be honest, years of carrying the bags and old injuries had definitely caught up with me, more so now that I was running. My main concern was my lower back and my knees, and if I'm going to have a real gripe, my teeth as well. After three of my molars were cracked in the Hebrides, they had become a constant pain drain as they began to rot; I kept a small bottle of whisky in my bag to swig, just so I could numb them to get to sleep. Abscess followed abscess, but to get the teeth replaced with implants would cost me a few thousand pounds and I just didn't have that kind of money. I had to put all of this to one side as I knew that looking after my family and getting this work done were more important than my physical issues. It was tiring me out so much that even my social media posts were becoming less frequent. Not only was I finding it hard to muster up the energy to post after such a tiring day, often just conking out in the evening, but the intensity of the running demanded a lot of my concentration and I was possibly missing a lot of what I would've normally picked up while I was walking to share on my page. Things like history videos and other videos that I'd loved doing so much were going out of the window.

Kate went to her mum's for the week to give me a chance to build up the miles and to make life easier for her with Magnus, rather than being constantly hosted by strangers. During that week, a lovely lady called Gaynor, who we had met while walking the Sussex Downs when Magnus was just three months old, got in touch with me. Thanks to her, a real sprinkle of joy landed on this little family. She had a holiday home in Penzance, not for rent, but for personal use, which she offered to us completely free of charge for three months. Under normal circumstances, we would never have taken her up on this, but we were desperate to be together again as a family, which meant we needed a base where Kate could recover and we were dead against Kate and Magnus spending their days picking me up and dropping me off in the van – that wasn't what we wanted for him. So the offer was absolutely incredible news for us.

23

The Scillies: a special birthday!

To give you an idea of the pace of the walk and how long it was taking us due to the logistics, and obviously me having to do double the mileage, it had taken us nine months to get from Hastings to the southwest corner of England. Ridiculous really, but it was simply testament to the level of challenge we were facing. The first few weeks of Kate being in Penzance, I was passing through places like Salcombe and Plymouth, heading towards Truro. The situation for Kate was hard; she was no longer able to continue the walk she loved so much and was in quite a lot of pain even pottering around. That March and April, it rained pretty much non-stop and, because Kate was without any transport of her own, she was confined to the house looking after a crawling toddler on her own all day. Like me, Kate had been looking forward to the southwest coast path for a long time now. She had never been to this part of the world either, and having missed out on the beauty of the west coast of Scotland and the Scottish islands, the south west was going to be some of the best coastline she had seen!

For the first two weeks or so, I was still too far away from Penzance to get home to them in the evenings and was still staying out in the van. I'd spent the day sprinting down the coast into Cornwall like a headless chicken trying to gain as much distance as I possibly could. I knew Kate wanted for us all to stay together as a family unit, and walking was her whole day, every day; it was her life. That said, she still got to spend all her time with Magnus, and for that, tiring as it could be sometimes, she was always grateful.

Finally, I made it to Truro, which was within driving distance of the Penzance home. I really enjoyed the entire section of this walk (run!), knowing that I could cuddle up with my baby boy along with Kate and Jet at the end of the day, without having to speak a word or talk about the walk! It was pure bliss! From around the Truro area, about an hour's drive east of Penzance, I was able to work my way along the coast, doing my normal running routine all the way up until we hit Newquay on the southwest coast, where we would be out of reaching distance from the house. During this time, Kate saw a few physios to help treat her injuries and was following advice when it came to exercises to help speed up her recovery as best she could.

Once I had reached Penzance, we would also get to

tackle what would be our last set of islands after nearly six years of walking. The Scilly Isles, without a shadow of a doubt, would turn out to be my favourite islands in England. They would also mark the end of an era. After these, never again on this walk would I get that feeling of heading to a British island I'd never been to before, and that wonderful excitement I've felt so many times when stepping from the boat to the jetty, taking a deep breath, ready to explore what was completely unknown to me. I was missing so much of this beautiful stretch of coastline and its rolling hills, craggy rocks and amazing little bays, because it was all about powering through – just run run run. This was the first time that reality had hit home that this walk would soon be done.

As it happened, I ended up going there initially with just my bergen and my dog, which made me nostalgic for all those times Jet and I had explored tiny islands back in Scotland, from Bute to Shetland. Kate's father, Ian, and stepmother, Val, had arranged to come for another visit to see Kate and their new grandson (and I would like to think me!), and had made an amazing effort, having flown all the way from Abu Dhabi. Our intention had been to head over to the islands as a family once Ian and Val had gone, but when Kate decided to have a quick look online at ferry availability and costs, it seemed the ferry was entirely booked up for weeks to come, as were any flights! There was only one date available for one passenger, and it just so happened to coincide with Ian and Val's visit. I knew Kate was desperate to make it out there, but we agreed that the most important thing was to ensure the Scillies got completed, so we booked me a ticket to go on my own with Jet and hoped that Kate and Magnus would be able to join me a few days later.

The Scilly Isles are a group of five inhabited islands, one of which is privately owned, and a cluster of unin-habited islets. As the flat-hulled ferry passed between the islands to get to St Mary's harbour, I saw beautiful white beaches and crystal-clear waters, and I remember thinking to myself, *Wow, this is as close to the Hebrides or Shetland that I have seen up until now!* I was really excited. I couldn't wait to get my teeth stuck into it.

When I first arrived on St Mary's, the main island, I was blown away by how beautiful it was. I picked up some supplies and headed to a small island that I noticed got cut off by the tide next to a beautiful white beach I'd been told about on the boat.

One thing I was pre-warned about even before stepping foot on the Scilly Isles was that wild camping was forbidden and it really annoyed some of the locals! But, given the fact that I was on my own, essentially homeless with a dog who struggled to walk far and with no van, as well as the fact that there was a huge gig (rowing boat) racing event going on and so everything was booked up, and knowing that this was my last island experience, I simply had no choice and thought, *Bollocks to it! Nothing and nobody is going to stop me from camping for at least a couple of nights on a small uninhabited island where I'm not doing anybody or anything any harm.*

By this point I found it hard to give a shit about these sorts of rules. I just had to do this, spend a few nights camped up on my tiny island when the tide was in. It was just me, Jet and a few oystercatchers. Looking back, I think I needed to just feel some freedom, if only for a couple of nights. I needed it for my own sanity and to recharge, ready to make my way back to Swansea.

You're not allowed to take vehicles over to the Scilly Isles – which suited me just fine. Being here took me back to the purer days of the walk, where it was just us and our bags. There was something liberating about it, and far more adventurous. Having managed to secure a few more ferry tickets, I knew Kate and Magnus would be joining me soon, and I missed them, but these few days on a beautiful island all to myself were so important for me. So much had happened in the three years before I met Kate, and so much had happened in the years after I'd met her. This was a real chance for me to just sit back, put my hands behind my head, lie on the soft heather and peaty ground of the tiny island, close my eyes and reflect. It was a special moment; it felt like the first time since leaving Hildasay that it was just me, the sound of the sea and the birds. *God*, I thought to myself, *this last bit has been tough! So tough! But soon enough, we will be able to choose where we want to go and reinstall that sense of epic adventure that I felt I had lost since leaving Scotland and losing the right to roam. One more big push, mate, one more big push and we're done.*

A few days later, Kate and Magnus joined me just in time for us to be able to celebrate Magnus's first birthday together on the islands, although it wasn't as simple as we'd hoped! Due to bad weather, all ferries and flights had been cancelled, meaning Kate and Magnus ended up scrambling to get on the only option left – a very small rib, for a total of five hours! Kate loved the journey at first but once the rain got to a point where she had to take Magnus inside, I began receiving messages saying that she was being sick as a pig over Magnus's shoulder while trying to hold on tight to him at the same time. I knew all too well what small boat crossings over choppy seas can be like, and I didn't envy her one bit as I sat sinking a nice pint in the local pub awaiting their arrival!

I'd already completed the most densely populated island, St Mary's, but during that time while I was wild camping on the tiny tidal island, my tent was flooded overnight with rain. A lovely lady called Fran, who had found out about me from a local community page, had come out with her dog to find me and offer help. She was married to the local harbour master, Dale, and the family had a small shed in the back garden with bedding and a few other bits that their eldest son used when he returned home from college. He was away at the time, so she offered it to me as a base. It was perfect timing, as Magnus and Kate were due to come out to the Scillies the next day.

Now, at the very end of April, the weather finally turning – a mix of downpours and brighter skies – we were soon blessed with a few days of fantastic weather.

We decided to mark Magnus turning one by spending a few days on the smaller, much quieter isle of St Martin's, which with its pristine white beaches couldn't have been more perfect.

Dale took us over the water on the official boat used for escorting the royal family when they came to stay, and as we sat playing on a vast stretch of empty white sand, a gentleman in his sixties named Tony, who lived on the island, turned up on his quad bike and said we could come and pitch the tent in the polytunnel in his garden and stay for as long as we liked.

Tony was a wonderful man; he lived very modestly and spent his days – in between caring for an elderly man whose land he was also in charge of maintaining – enjoying the sanctuary and peace of living on such a small island. At night after our day's walking, we would have dinner with him, and he went out of his way to make us incredible meals followed by a good jam on the guitar. We would sit singing, laughing and dancing together until it was time to retire to the polytunnel. We couldn't have chosen a more idyllic place to spend our son's first birthday, and we relished the simple joy of having fun together, playing on the sand, dipping in and out of the freezing crystal-clear waters, taking a tour of the island all squashed in the back of Tony's quad-bike trailer – all washed down with a beautiful sunset! It was perfect.

We were really taking our time to enjoy it as we slowly made our way around the island. In smaller stints, Kate even managed to walk the island herself, which I know gave her a real sense of satisfaction too.

Having left St Martin's, we arrived on the smaller island of Bryher, some 2 nautical miles to the west, and were invited to stay free of charge at the only campsite for the duration of our time there. It was the beginning of

May and the island was pretty much empty of tourists. We carried on the birthday celebrations, enjoying the sugar-white beaches, collecting an abundance of different-coloured shells to show to Magnus, and just marvelling at beautiful scenery and the incredible views over the surrounding islands from the top of Bryher's hills. Having these little beaches to ourselves was pure bliss, and just what we needed. Bryher had the wildest feel of all the islands and really was beautiful. It was a very special time and the islands felt unique; a slice of paradise that we were thrilled to experience on our journey. Kate also managed to walk the whole of Bryher pain-free over a few days. It had been such a long time since Kate and I had felt so relaxed, and we enjoyed each other's company with far fewer stresses in a much quieter place. Finally, we could take a step back and just be a little family for a while.

Because of the nature of our journey and how we were having to do it, Kate and I would often laugh and joke that the last time we'd had a cuddle in bed together was before Kate became too heavily pregnant. The difficulty we had found trying to wild camp as a family meant always having to sleep separately. Even in the house in Penzance, Jet and I always ended up staying in a different room, as Kate co-slept with Magnus. We'd never had room in the van for a travel cot, and the nature of us all sleeping in a tiny van or in the tent meant Magnus always slept alongside us. With Jet insistent on sleeping by my side as well, there was never any room for Kate and me to be close!

It's really funny how a simple rule like 'no camping' can have such an effect on nomads like us! In a strange way, although we were together all the time, Kate and I were actually living separate lives. I missed her and I missed our evening fun, just chatting, laughing and playing games. I craved the day when little Magnus could be sleeping by our side, with Jet nestled between our feet, and Kate and I would be able to have a cuddle just like any couple would.

Some people might look at our photos of idyllic coastal landscapes and think that all of this was just sunshine and rainbows, but believe me, it wasn't. As I'm sure would be the same for any couple that are together 24/7 with a young baby, things did get tense between myself and Kate at times. She is a strong-willed woman in every aspect of her life, and there's absolutely no difference when it comes to an argument, but I think it's fair to say she's met her match with me, as I'm also the kind of guy who won't back down if I believe I'm right! Back on the mainland, the money situation, stress for both of us linked to Kate's injury, and my desperation to get this walk completed for all of our sakes had led to the occasional disagreement! This is one of the reasons the Scilly Isles were so special to us, added to the fact that they were the last group of islands we'd visit and also Magnus's birthday. Just being there together was like pressing a family reset button – in fact it felt like a family holiday before our final push back to Swansea.

After completing Tresco, the only privately owned island in the Scillies, our very last island was St Agnes.

It was a short boat trip. From the very first moment that Kate and I met and all the way through our relationship, I'd never stopped talking about how much I loved islands and how they had been the absolute highlight of my personal adventure. Obviously, we could go to more after the walk finished, but I would no longer get that exciting feeling of unpredictability and wonder as to what the next one had to offer. I thought about it a lot and probably talked about it a lot without realizing, and I think Kate sensed a real sadness in me. I know Kate loved the islands as well and was desperate to go to St Agnes, our next and final island, but as we made our way on the small passenger boat back to St Mary's, where we would catch another yet boat to take us to St Agnes, she said, 'It's okay, Chris – why don't you just go over on your own and spend the night there in your tent, just you. It's the last of your islands. Just go by yourself with Jet and give yourself a chance to take it all in and have some time alone.'

I knew how much Kate wanted to go, so I really appreciated her selflessness and promised her we'd return together one day in the future. While Kate and Magnus went back to the cabin at Dale and Fran's, I jumped on the little ferry over and Jet and I walked the mile to the campsite right next to the sea and started putting up the tent. However, as is often the case with island weather, another storm hit and that evening before nightfall my tent pole snapped! Any other time, I would've been gutted, but I remember just looking at the tent pole with a smile. God, I'd worked so hard around all those islands in

Scotland, all the winters, springs, autumns and summers; all the broken tents and poundings we would get from the cold, wet winter weather. And here I was on my last island, back in my tent, and it just all seemed so fitting! With a gust of wind on a southern isle in May, my tent (which had been battered to destruction on the northern isles) said it's goodbyes for the last time on the walk. By now, the sky had calmed and cleared again, and I walked down to the seafront for about half an hour and just looked out to sea without muttering a word.

It was such a special little moment; only I knew what it had taken to finish the islands of the United Kingdom. I thought a lot about all the people who had helped along the way and all of the islands that I'd walked. Each one had a very different, more relaxed way of living; far friendlier and with a tight-knit sense of togetherness that filled me with hope, knowing it still existed in some parts of the UK. How privileged and lucky I felt to have seen this for myself and been part of so many amazing island traditions, from Shetland's 'Up Helly' to when I was a torch bearer for the memorial of the *Iolaire* for all those soldiers returning from war who lost their lives in the most tragic of shipwrecks, and so close to home.

I thought about how these islands had accepted an outsider, someone who had first arrived a complete stranger but who had left feeling so loved and so welcomed. I thought about the beautiful wildlife, the incredible scenery and those once-in-a-lifetime moments I'd had that would stay with me for ever; like when I was in Jura, sharing a cave with a deer and sheep; watching golden eagles and sea eagles soar above me as we traversed the mountains of Scotland; and Christmases and birthdays spent on uninhabited islands that were mind-blowingly beautiful. But most importantly of all, it was the alone time in the wilderness that helped me to rekindle my sense of purpose in life, and for that reason alone they are and will always remain the most special places I have ever been to.

While I had my hands in my pockets and my hat very loosely on top of my head, out of nowhere the winds picked up, blowing the hat from my head for the first time in as long as I can remember, exposing my hair and forehead to the fresh air. I just stood there with it off for a few minutes and closed my eyes. It was such a peaceful and fulfilling moment. I picked up my hat from the floor and gave Jet a stroke on the top of her head.

'Goodbye for now, islands, thank you so much for helping me, even if you had no idea that you did. I promise you, I'll be back again and this time with my little family right by my side all the way. Until then, my friends.' With that, I made my way back for my final night's sleep in a broken tent on St Agnes.

With the Scilly Isles now in the bag, it was time to head back to the mainland. The ferry company had very kindly offered us free return passage, which was fantastic for us, given that travel here wasn't cheap. The Clark family all came to see us off as we boarded, and Kate even had tears in her eyes as we left. She had really loved it here. We took a deep breath as we stood on the decking on the back of the boat waving goodbye.

As we pulled out of the harbour, Tony suddenly appeared speeding alongside our ferry in a small rib to see us off! It was so funny watching him bounce airborne over the waves in the wake of our huge ferry, trying to keep control as he literally flew over the waves. It was a lovely touch on his part and a great way to be waved off by someone who'd played such a big part in making our stay so memorable: a great finale to our island adventure! Our boat ride back was topped off by a pod of dolphins diving alongside us in the distance. I'd always loved the adventure of boat crossings, and I did find it funny that on the ferries down south, customers go to the bar on board and ask for things like Earl Grey tea and scones, whereas in the Hebrides and Shetland it was, 'Give me a double whisky and a couple of cans of Tennent's'!

24

The end of the odyssey

As soon as we arrived back on the mainland, I got to work immediately, running to Land's End. It only took me a few days, but when we finally got there, Kate and Magnus joined Jet and me to stand next to the post that signified that we had reached the southwest corner of England! As I made for the post, passing a little hut with two people sitting inside, the woman shouted, 'Excuse me!'

I turned to see what the commotion was. 'If you want to stand next to the sign then you have to pay a fee and it's more expensive if you want a photo taken next to it!'

'Are you kidding?' I argued. 'Nearly six years of walking the UK coastline and this is the first time that I've ever been charged for standing next to a piece of wood! I don't have any money. I'm doing this walk for charity,' I explained.

'Well, then, you'll have to wait until we are gone after 4 p.m. when we take most of the signs down, but you can still get a photo next to it.'

'That's three hours away!' I said. 'Surely anybody should have the right to stand on a tiny piece of land that signifies the southwest point!'

As I say – everything here seems so monetized. Slightly deflated, I sat on the very southwest tip of England. I knew that in two weeks' time, I'd be far enough up the west coast of England that I'd be able to see home for the first time in just under six years. What a moment that would be!

The weather really had changed now, and the days were already starting to get hot, too hot for Jet to be sitting in the van during the heat of the day, so we had to go back to the routine that we'd adopted on previous summers throughout the journey. I would wake up at 5 o'clock every morning and sink my two cups of coffee inside the van, and as soon as that sun started to rise, I put my shoes on, left Jet in the van and went for it! Kate and Magnus were still staying in Penzance for now, so I would continue as before, running from one car park to another, there and back again before driving to where I'd got to and repeating the same process again, and again, and again!

By now we'd realized that having to pay for National Trust and Europcar car parks (among others) was costing us a fortune – sometimes around £65–75 a day alone, and that's not to mention the number of fines we got for me being late back after having to run unfamiliar and steep terrain. It was absolutely ridiculous! Essentially, for walking the coastline of the UK for charity, I was now paying a National Trust employee's daily wage to park my van. It was soul-destroying. It came to a point when I'd arrive at the car parks and would literally beg the National Trust assistant and say, 'Please, mate, I'm only going to be here for an hour. I'm walking the UK coastline for charity and just can't afford to keep paying these parking prices.'

But never once was I given even the slightest bit of leeway. Along with this and the copious amounts of land owned by the National Trust, which offers limited access to the general public, I would often wonder how on earth a charity had become so powerful and basically in a position where it can dictate so much when it comes to land access.

By the time I'd made it round to Newquay, Kate and Magnus had left our temporary home in Penzance to rejoin me full-time; the weather was really warm and we had decided to go back to staying in campsites to make the most of being outside. The more I got my teeth stuck into the southwest coast path, the more gutted I was that we couldn't all wild camp together. In my eyes, it was by far the most beautiful England had to offer, and the north Cornish coast was really spectacular.

With very little around in the way of major towns, I worked my way over beautiful steep sea cliffs and rolling green hills with plenty of golden beaches showcasing some great surf. Every now and then, I'd pass the most quaint, beautiful little villages. It really was gorgeous, and I was gutted not to be spending more time exploring and seeing more of this place. Kate was doing a bit better and would walk sections, but we were conscious she shouldn't do too much in case it set her back. At the end of the day, we felt the sacrifice on her part for the rest of this adventure was worth it if it meant she'd be back to full physical health for the next one. As for me, I was genuinely happy when the weather turned and it rained, keeping the masses of tourists at bay. My word, it was gobsmacking just how many people visited these parts this early in the tourist season, St Ives in particular! I was in and out of there like a shot – pretty as I could see it was underneath the crowds, the mass of tourists and holiday homes just weren't for me. As I stood at the top of each hill that led down into a small village or town, it was like looking upon a swarm of bees!

I thought to myself, *These poor locals – they go through the whole winter waiting for the days where they can go out and fully enjoy the place only to be swamped by tourists!* Not even so much of a parking space was free from the early hours, and queueing up for a coffee was a waste of half a day. I suppose that's the price you pay for living somewhere so pretty. I thought of Scotland; the sheer distance and amount of time it took to drive up there, along with the unpredictable weather and summer midges, kept a lot of would-be visitors at bay. Ironically, my old nemesis was the area's saviour when it came to tourists.

In spite of the tourists, I knew I wouldn't be hitting a coastline this beautiful again on this walk, and so I made the most of it and took nice long breaks in quiet places on the coast path to take it all in and prepare myself for crossing that line, which seemed impossible for my brain to fathom. I just couldn't get it into my head that this was all going to be over in a few months.

At the start of July we headed into North Devon, I continued running, and we had some of the best weather of the entire summer. We found as many quiet spots in larger campsites by the coast as we could, but as the temperatures rose, it made things a lot trickier with Jet. I would have to get up at around 4.30 a.m. to leave by 5 a.m. at the latest to ensure I covered my morning miles before it got too hot to leave Jet in the van. This meant I would often sleep out in the van as close as I could to my starting point for the following day and leave Kate and Magnus camping on their own. Kate was an experienced camper now and I was never worried on that front, but I always felt guilty being away from them so much. Once I'd done my morning miles, I would head back to them for some family time during my break, while Jet had a potter around or a spot of sunbathing, and I helped Kate pack up our gear if we were moving campsite again. During the day, Kate would spend time with Magnus in the various bays along my route – his knees must have crawled over nearly every beach on that southwest coast path!

As I headed towards the Severn Bridge, I arrived in a place called Lynton, around 50 miles from the border of England and Wales. It had been a misty, busy day with quite a bit of wind, and the sea mist rolled over the cliff tops, making for a nice cool day for running, a very welcome change, enabling me to get more miles in without worrying about Jet getting too hot in the van. Then, as I stood high up on the top of a sea cliff, as if somebody had clicked their fingers, a bright blue sky appeared out of nowhere! With the warmth of the sun on my face – like Odysseus having been lost at sea for ten years, and away in the Trojan war for another decade, when he finally spots his island of Ithaca in the distance – I suddenly saw Llangennith!

It was around 30 miles west of the Severn estuary – Llangennith beach, the place where I'd first started from, five years and nine months ago. My heart started to beat faster as I stood there working my eyes slowly along the first stretch of familiar land all walk. I could make out all the beaches along the coast to Llangennith, including Caswell, Langland, and of course Swansea Bay. To the right of Swansea, I could see the steelworks and the steam coming from Port Talbot. What a moment this was; I couldn't believe what I was seeing!

Memories of the very first day came flooding back, and of my days surfing on all these beaches, of me and Caitlin, and of course, of how I felt the last time I saw this place. *God*, I thought to myself, *who would've known that the next time I would see this, I'd have a dog, a fiancée and another child!* I know I'd found this last couple of years difficult, but it's like anything in life – you just have to take the good with the bad, a mentality that I had lost before I set off.

'What an adventure!' I muttered to myself. 'What a bloody adventure!'

I was sad that I'd been wishing away the last part of it, but the circumstances had made things tricky. We felt that if we were really going to do right by Jet, we would've had to sit out the peak of summer for her sake and restart when it got cooler if we didn't get a shift on. The previous August had seen a very uncomfortable heatwave, and it would have been so difficult with Jet if the same happened this year. It would be less than ideal with Magnus, too. I was also desperate to get Kate back up and running and fighting-fit once again. I wanted nothing more than for Jet to put her paws up and for us all to be together all the time.

That aside, I have no real words to describe how sad I was going to be once that line was crossed, knowing that this lifestyle I'd been living for so long, and that had given me so many incredible experiences along the way, would come to an end just like that. For one, I would no longer need to be checking my maps a hundred times a day from the first minute I woke to the last thing before bed. Our lives were about to change. As a family, we were ready for it, but on a personal level I found the thought of this change really difficult. This was going to sting, I knew. 'Chris Walks the UK' would be over – finished! It had been my life for so long and, looking across the water at Swansea, I knew I had to accept that very soon we would be done.

One thing that really struck me while I stared over at Swansea was that not at any point did I ever say to myself, 'There's home!' That word 'home' for some reason just didn't seem or feel right to me. It didn't give me that feeling of warmth and contentment or even excitement that one should feel after such a long endeavour. I realized in this moment that the meaning of the word 'home' had become something completely different to me. It was no longer a place, nor the stones, brick walls or interiors that make up a house. Our journey throughout England and the circumstances that had led me to spend more time away from Kate, Magnus and Jet had taught me probably the most valuable of life's lessons: it didn't matter where I was sleeping; the only time that I felt truly at home was when Kate, Magnus, Jet and Caitlin were by my side. We could be anywhere in the world so long as we were together. Only then was I home. I didn't need anything else; no big posh house, fancy cars, or any material things for that matter. Thank God I had broken free from believing that these are the things that make us happy. If anything, they pull you away from the very foundations that made us all thrive in the first place – a distraction from what is genuinely important: the people we love.

I knew full well that I wouldn't be staying in Swansea very long, a few weeks at most. There was far too much out there to stay in one place for the rest of our lives. With the understanding that my family was my home, I knew that wherever I went, my home would come with me. That was the amazing thing about finding such a like-minded partner in Kate. The end of this walk wouldn't mean me carving a new path in adventure while she was left behind with Magnus; no, she was coming with me. Whatever we would do next, we would do together, and that was how we imagined our future. I had realized that the only thing of any value that I wanted to grow around me were people that I loved. Everything else can stay sat on the shelves to collect dust!

By now, I had set a date for the finish line, to give people who might want to come to witness the end of the walk enough notice, as well as those who were helping to organize the day. It would be 29 July 2023, almost six years to the day that I set off on 1 August 2017. In order to feel 100 per cent safe in the knowledge that we were going to make it in time, I did my best to pick up the pace as we came to our last and final section of England, which would take us in and around the outskirts of Bristol and finally to the Severn Bridge.

I was exhausted by this point. The weather was getting hotter by the day; the ridiculously early mornings and late nights of running, combined with constantly trying to figure out a way for Kate and Magnus to be near me more often, were really taking their toll. Extremely long days, which revolved around thinking, planning and running back and forth from car park to car park for months on end had tired me out! With these being much more densely populated areas, Kate and Magnus were now staying in spare rooms offered by kind people who wanted to help us out on this stretch. It was certainly tiring for Kate on her own with Magnus nearly all day and then staying in a different house with him each night, but on the plus side, she enjoyed meeting lots of interesting people and Magnus was getting plenty of social interaction. He was so adaptable by this point; nothing fazed him! He was the most relaxed, happy little boy and it was clear for anyone to see that he was reaping the benefits of his outdoor lifestyle.

Arriving at the Severn Bridge was a monumental moment, with a multitude of people coming to see us over and cross back into Wales, congratulating us, asking questions and taking photos. I remember feeling so over-whelmed and all-around just knackered! Bless Kate, I knew she was essentially raising Magnus on her own at this point and I felt like I was letting her down, but I also knew that I was doing everything that I possibly could to get us over the finish line. It weighed heavily on my mind as I sprinted my way across the coastline each day.

I had thought about crossing the bridge on so many occasions and how I might feel at such a monumental moment on this journey, and on a personal level it was epic. However, my mind had been so consumed with worry about Kate and Jet, and where we were going to go after we finished the walk, that I struggled to enjoy it as much as I'd envisaged. By now, I'd already signed a deal for my second book, and the deadline was the end of August, which left me only six weeks, some of which would still be on the walk as we geared up for the finish. How the hell was I going to do it? The last one took me three months, and I didn't think it could get much harder than writing with a newborn while still on the walk. This time round, however, the circumstances seemed even harder! Somehow, I had to cover around 20 miles a day, find a way to be there for Kate, find somewhere to stay temporarily after we finished the walk, and bang out a book! *Jesus!* I thought. Deep down, though, I knew I'd been in far worse positions. And if anyone could do it, I could. Just like with the walk, failing was not an option.

There were strong winds the day we crossed, and being high up on a bridge that was 2 miles long with the deafening noise of traffic zooming past, we knew that Magnus and Jet would hate it. So we came up with a Plan B, which entailed my mum (who had come up to see us over the bridge) taking Kate, Magnus and Jet over to the Welsh side, where they would wait and then come and meet me for the last stretch of the bridge. Left on my own now, I took a deep breath and started to jog from the service station and along the path that runs by the side of the old bridge.

As I ran, I saw a crowd of people lined up clapping as I went past. Suddenly, everything else just disappeared and I started to really focus on the moment and the enormity of stepping back into the country where I first started that had seemed so far away for so long. I stopped pretty much exactly halfway across the bridge and just looked over at the River Severn at the section I had just finished in England, and the section I was just about to do in Wales. This was my moment. At the top of my voice and with my eyes welling up with self-pride and achieve-ment, I screamed, 'Yes!' as loud as I possibly could.

I turned back around and started running over the hump of the bridge where I could see a crowd and a Channel 4 News camera crew waiting, as well as Kate carrying Magnus with Jet by her side, about a hundred yards from the crossing into Wales. Together with Kate, our little boy on her back and Jet by my side, and after five years, eleven months and two weeks, I stepped foot on the soil of the country where I had first started. What a feeling indeed.

We now had two weeks until the end of the walk on

29 July, so Kate, Magnus, Jet and I started heading eagerly towards Swansea. It was only around 60 miles and very easy coastline.

I turned to Kate: 'Babe, we've nearly done it! I'm so proud of us. Fuck, this has been hard!'

And she replied: 'Chris, you should be so proud of yourself; as much of a grumpy pain in the arse you have been in the past year, only we will know how hard it's been, but we're nearly there. By hook or by crook, remember – never give up!'

I smiled. 'Never.'

I pushed hard and fast, running my socks off to get us down towards Swansea as quickly as possible. God only knows how many messages I had from people who wanted to come and say hello as I passed through places like Cardiff, Porthcawl and Port Talbot, but I just wanted to do this section on my own without any distractions. I remember reaching Port Talbot and parking up in a spot we had always used whenever we'd go surfing in this area at Margam. It suddenly dawned on me that there might be quite a few people at this finish line! *How on earth am I going to take any of it in?* I thought. I'd craved so much that moment of silence stood on the top of Rhossili cliffs, where I first had the epiphany to walk the UK coastline. I needed that, and I knew I wasn't going to get it around a crowd of people.

Kate and Magnus at this point were staying between my good friend Alan Pugh's house, my other good friend Chris Carree's and my mother's, to make life easier for her with Magnus at night, because it was raining non-stop for days on end. So, it was just me and Jet. I had around a week to walk the rest of the coast, but running it would only take me a few days, so I could arrive early and give myself some time to process it all. There was a voice in my head telling me, *Just go, mate, just go and see it! Have your moment alone, with no distractions! Fucking hell, it's been six years, you deserve at least that much.*

And with that, I drove to Swansea without telling anybody. I can't tell you how strange that was driving through Swansea City. Every path and every road that I saw was a memory. I passed the Civic Centre, thinking to myself, *My God, mate, the last time you saw this place, you came out in tears after begging for more time to pay off some rent you owed, to no joy.* I recalled that sinking, soul-destroying feeling that homelessness was on the imminent horizon. When stricken with it, anxiety becomes your whole world; it feels like there's no escaping from it. So, every nook and cranny of the city felt like a bad memory; it was quite sad really. But here I was six years later, a completely different man, and although exhausted, I couldn't help but smile at how I'd changed my life and the fact that I had done it all myself.

At the end of the day, it was me who found the strength to pull myself out of my hole, and no one else. I had grabbed life by the horns and refused to quit until I was in charge of that saddle! As I looked around at Swansea City, I realized that nothing here had changed; it was all the same. The only thing that *had* changed was me.

25

Back to where I started

At around 4 p.m. that afternoon, I arrived at Rhossili car park unable to work out if seeing the finish line before I had finished was a good idea. I sat back in the T4 and looked over at Jet, who was lying down in the back. 'Hey, Jet, this is where I'm from, pal. Do you want to come and see it with me?' As I opened the door, she jumped up, her tail wagging as ever with her usual look of 'what's next, Dad?'

We both walked slowly towards the cliff tops, with me hoping that I wouldn't be recognized so I could just have this moment in peace. Fortunately, there weren't many people about as we slithered like a couple of sneaky criminals to the grassy knoll that overlooked Llangennith and the very spot I'd stood on six years ago.

I had pictured this moment so many times, and

wondered how I would feel when I saw it. Would I jump up in the air with joy to be back? Would I burst into tears knowing that I'd achieved what I'd set out to do? Or would I be panicking, thinking, *What on earth are you going to do next?* There were so many potential scenarios that had played through my mind over the years but, in the end, none of them turned out to be the case.

From the grassy knoll, I focused my sights on the old shipwreck that pokes its nose out of the sand on a low tide, and the same spot where I'd come out of the sea grateful to be alive after riding such a massive swell before I left. I thought about Caitlin and how perhaps she would never know just how much she had saved my life. She'd given me a purpose and a reason to keep going and I was so proud of her for stepping foot into the big wide world at such a young age, having the courage to leave me to better her own life.

I thought about Kate and Magnus and how much they had brought to my life. They were my second chance; another shot at being a good dad, a family man. They were my biggest adventure on the walk and now I would be with them for the rest of my life. I thought of Jet, who had been my constant through everything, my calm in the eye of the storm, always there by my side, so loyal and precious. A simple look from her always made me feel amazing no matter what the situation. I'd often joke to Kate and say, 'If I locked you in the boot of a car with Jet for six hours, I guarantee only one of you would jump for joy to see me!', to which she would always reply, 'You're damn right!' That's the love of a dog.

I'd thought reaching the end was going to be the ultimate prize, but how wrong I was. As I looked down at the finish line on the beach, it suddenly dawned on me that it was now time to grab life by the horns once again and start a new adventure. With Kate by my side, whatever it was we decided we wanted to do next, no matter how ridiculous it may sound to anybody else, we would make it work. Here I was standing in the same spot where I'd once felt like the whole world was against me. As I stood here now, I knew that the world was mine with which to do whatever I wanted; to do what was going to make me and my family happy in the stupidly short time we have here.

Coming back to where I had started had shown me one thing: I had chosen freedom over material wealth. Before the walk, I had tried to chase the same life as so many others, and I'd failed miserably because I simply wasn't invested in the idea. That conveyor belt of rules and the hemmed-in box of societal expectations dictating how life should be lived didn't fit with who I was, and it was this that drove me to rock bottom. I'd put in thirty-seven years to this way of doing things, and to no avail. Then one day, I decided to step out of the shadows of the rat race and take a chance on something regardless of how totally mental, ludicrous, unplanned or disorganized it seemed. I'd made a call on a total whim. That's adventure – that's what I love doing! And it had all started here.

I stayed in this spot, contemplating the significance of this ending for forty minutes or so, before heading back towards the van with a huge smile on my face. It couldn't be truer when they said that it's not the destination but the journey it takes to get there that matters. That's the adventure, the prize if you like.

Finally, the moment had come. Time to officially cross the line and finish the walk! There had been a lot of preparation that had gone into the finish, and SSAFA had been absolutely instrumental in making sure that it was all perfect for us; what an effort they put in! The finish line had been arranged in Hill End Caravan Park where the owner had cut a nice section of grass on which we would cross the finish line when we came through the sand dunes at Llangennith.

The first order of events that day was to start at Rhossili Bay, where we had invited anyone who wanted to come to meet us and walk the final mile with us down the cliffs and along the beach to the finish. We were absolutely gobsmacked at the sea of people who had already turned up ready to join us on our final mile! It was incredible, and I couldn't have wished for a better turnout. Before we left the van, Jet, Kate, Magnus and I had a little minute to ourselves. There was a lot of press and inter- views that we had to do before leaving and we were getting pushed to get them done as they were all operating on a timescale, but I didn't care. This was our moment and anything else could wait as far as I was concerned. I gave Kate and Jet a huge hug and said, 'Thank you for being by my side for so much of this journey,' and told them how proud I was of both of them. I could feel I was starting to well up, but I knew I had to hold myself together.

I was so grateful I had taken that moment at Rhossili before the day of the finish line to come and see it for myself. It was a good choice. We walked up to the crowd awaiting our arrival and everybody stood to the side clapping and cheering us on. It was wonderful. I could see tears starting to form in Kate's eyes. This would soon be over for her too, after nearly three years. Whether they were tears of joy or sadness, I didn't know, but either way, it was a remarkable moment for her as well. Jet, on the other hand, was as ever doing her utmost to keep out of the crowd and avoid the noise, constantly dragging on the lead. *Bless her*, I thought. 'Don't worry, mate,' I said. 'It'll be over soon.'

Before we left for the final mile, the crowd gathered round in a semicircle as we stood by the fence near the cliff edges next to the path that let down to the beach for some formalities. Sir Andrew Gregory, head of SSAFA, was there to greet us and give a speech. It was at this moment that we found out we had not only hit but surpassed our £500,000 target! As well as through my JustGiving page, the donations had been pouring in to SSAFA directly for our cause and someone in London was tallying up the total, letting Sir Andrew know that the half-million mark had been hit! What a feeling! After everything my family and I had been through to raise that money, we were over the moon, and we knew that we had earned every penny of it.

Other military personnel were also there, and I was really touched that they had made the effort, especially a group of ten Paras who had come down to do the final mile with us. It meant so much to me. Also present was the Lord Lieutenant, smartly dressed in her number ones, who delivered another lovely speech congratulating us on our achievements. I couldn't believe it when she pulled out a letter from the King of England, who wanted to thank me for my efforts in fundraising for such a worthy cause. What an honour! *Fucking hell*, I thought, as she was reading out the letter, *I really didn't think I'd be getting letters from the King of England when I first started!* And nor, for that matter, did I believe that the sea of people that I was staring at would be so big, and that this day would have such an all-around wonderful, warm vibe. I was blown away. The Lord Mayor of Swansea was also there and when he came over to chat, he asked if there was anything he could do now I was back in Swansea. 'Please let me know,' he said.

I turned to him and said, 'As it goes, I think I probably have some outstanding council tax – any chance that paperwork could be conveniently lost?' As I laughed, he did too.

'I'll see what I can do!' he said.

'Perfect. Cheers, mate!'

People had travelled from all over the UK to come and support us at this moment, even as far as Unst, our nation's most northerly isle – and that is some journey! We were so touched. Before we headed towards the line, we were dragged off to do some press interviews and a radio interview with Carol Vorderman live on her show! To be honest, it was all a bit of a blur as the only thing that was in my mind was taking that final step with my little family. Once I'd finished, we started to make our way down the cliffs to the beach of Rhossili with myself, Kate, Magnus and Jet leading from the front. When we arrived at the bottom, we both turned to look back. It was mind-blowing to see the number of people still coming from the top and processing down to the beach, all of them here to see us! I just couldn't believe what this walk had amounted to and what it had obviously meant to so many people. Kate and I looked on in amazement. 'It's really happening; we are actually finishing!' I kept telling myself.

Brian, a good friend who we'd met on the walk, had come all the way from Newcastle with huge flags of all the countries that I had walked, mounted to big wooden poles that were carried behind us as we made our way down the beach. Onlookers who didn't know what was happening later commented that as we traversed Llangennith beach for that last mile, we looked like an army of Vikings who had come to invade! We were all cocooned together in one mass gathering with close to a thousand people who had come down to support, all surrounding us closely. All the while, I was being so protective over Jet as well as an elderly lady called Ann Savage-Lewis, an avid follower who I'd been in touch with on and off since near to the very beginning and who was standing beside us. People were running up, asking for autographs and for us to sign copies of my book, as well as endless selfies! It was just insane; it all didn't seem real! When we got to the last bit, which was a walk through a narrow sandy pass into Hill End campsite where the finish line was, we asked everyone to make their way to the finish line so that Kate, Jet, Magnus and I could just have a minute to ourselves to take it all in.

Just then, out of the blue, my book editor, Richard, turned up. I was so delighted to see him, having formed the most wonderful relationship with him during the whole writing process. I can safely say I can now call him my friend and I was really chuffed to see him. After a quick chat, it was time to do our last few hundred yards! With the banners flying high behind us, we made our way through the sandy track and soon enough the finish line came into sight! I turned to give Kate a big kiss. 'We've done it, babe, we've actually done it! Can you believe it?' I said as she looked at me with the most loving eyes and a huge smile on her face as she welled up.

With all my friends, family and all the followers who had travelled from afar clapping and cheering us on, we made our way to the finish line held up by SSAFA crew and military personnel. The crowd were lined on either side, cheering and clapping as loud as you can imagine with Kate and myself holding Magnus's hands as he walked, and Jet stood right next to me. As we looked ahead, through the sea of phone cameras and the flashes of press photographers all snapping away at this moment, together we crossed the finish line. I remember my head just tilting back and screaming 'yes!' at the top of my voice, through the noise of all the clapping and cheering. It was so special and such a once-in-a-lifetime moment. We had done it.

Six years ago, I set out to walk the entire UK coastline

to rediscover myself and to raise money for charity, and I made a promise to myself that I would return a happy man. I had succeeded and more. Without a doubt, it had been the journey of a lifetime, my own personal pilgrimage that had led to great things. And it was done, finally in the bag. It was one of the best moments in my life and I will never ever forget it.

The Kings Head pub in Llangennith (my favourite pub in all of the Gower, which I would often visit after a day of surfing or working – my local if you like) had gone above and beyond to make this day great. They had decorated the inside and outside of the pub with homemade bunting that had been sent by people from all four corners of the UK thanks to a creative idea of Kate's! It was just amazing seeing the effort that people had put in, knowing they couldn't be there but in some way wanting to be part of this day nonetheless. There was also a huge flag pinned to the back of the pub, with a picture of Jet and me printed all over it, which read, 'Welcome Home'. There were food vans and bands during the day as well as live music in the evening and a pub full of lovely happy people ready to share a few beers with us and celebrate our six-year triumph! It really was incredible.

When I got to the pub, I was itching to sink a pint and take the edge off what had so far been a busy and emotional day, but instead I found myself unable to even get near the entrance and faced with a queue of people with books in their hands asking me to sign them and get some selfies. I really didn't mind this at all, and was so happy to give people my time given the effort they had made for us on this day. Realizing that everybody else had eaten except for me, the manager of the pub, Laura, dragged me away to one side and sat me behind a burger van out of sight of anybody so that I could just gulp one down. It really was crazy! Everything had gone so well and the whole place was buzzing.

As the evening started drawing in, I'd spent much of it without even a sip of Guinness, chatting away to people, answering questions and signing books. I didn't even get to speak to my family, and I was really starting to get tired. I had planned to sing a song for everybody, but I was just too spent – overwhelmed, I think would be the word! Magnus was now sleeping in the hotel room that had been given to us for free that night by the pub, while Kate watched him. I sneaked off and walked upstairs to the bedroom.

'Kate, I really need a rest. You go down and enjoy your-self and see your mum, dad and the rest of your family. I'll just stay here with Magnus.'

Kate agreed and, given that Magnus was now walking, she'd been racing around with him and hadn't had a chance to catch up with friends or family yet. I cuddled up with my arm wrapped around a sleeping Magnus, thinking how beautiful he was. Jet nestled down at the bottom of my feet with her head poking up, leaning over my ankle so that she could have eyes on me.

With all the lights turned off, and the door still open to allow the fresh air in, of all the moments of the day, this was the most special. I finally had a chance to take a deep breath and inhale it; all my family and Kate's family, friends that I knew from Swansea, friends that I'd made on the walk and people that I'd never even met before who had come to support us – they were all down in the pub having a wonderful time together. The music was pumping out and I could hear the laughing and chattering clearly from my room. Such a warm and lovely feeling came over me. I didn't need to be part of it to enjoy it! I was happy to just sit back and spectate. I was really proud that, somehow, this journey had brought all of these people together, and only a few yards from the hotel room. I laid my head back and closed my eyes. I'd done it.

'Well in, fella!' I muttered to myself, and fell asleep next to Jet and Magnus.

'Chris Walks the UK' was over.

26

Laying old haunts to rest

With the walk now done and everybody gone, I had to make an immediate transition with only four weeks left to write my next book about the final three years of this walk and figure out a way to get this all done. Although the walk was finished, it really didn't feel like it, as we would spend the next week moving from place to place, finding somewhere to sleep and doing press interviews to try to boost that final fundraising total as much as we could.

Understandably, my friends and family all wanted us to visit and go and see them but knowing how much pressure I was under and how much work I had to do, as much as I wanted to, I just didn't have time. The camping laws in Wales forbidding room to roam are exactly the same as in England and, given that it was now the height of the summer season, there was no way in this world I could sit in a busy campsite writing a book. I just wanted to be somewhere on my own where I could have a fire and get on with it. After about a week of having hardly got anything done, I sat down with Kate.

'Darling, there's absolutely no way that I can get this book done where we are, just no way.'

To my huge surprise, my last book had become a *Sunday Times* bestseller; it had done well! I really didn't want to do the rest of the journey an injustice by being so rushed in my writing about it, which was inevitably turning out to be the case. The only way I had any chance of finishing was to pull myself away from everything and everyone and just get it done.

'Where do you want to go?' she asked.

'Back to Scotland, so at least I can be free, and I think it will do me good to go up on my own with Jet and just process this all being over. I feel like I need to do that before I can put pen to paper.'

'Okay, you go for it,' she said. 'I'll stay here with my mum in Malvern to give you a chance.'

As much as all I wanted to do was be with my family having now finished the walk, my work was far from over!

That night, I packed the van and, with Jet, travelled back up to Scotland. As we crossed the border into the country of Robert the Bruce, I said to Jet, 'Pal, look, we could pitch a tent over there if you want and they wouldn't say anything – what a feeling! It's been years since I knew we could do that.'

In a strange way, I had almost the same feeling as when

I'd first stepped foot in Scotland all those years ago. It felt unbelievably generous that we could do this! On my first night back in Scotland, I drove to exactly the same spot on the south coast near Annan where, years before, I had suffered my coldest night in all of the walk after stupidly allowing my sleeping bag to get soaked, when, ironically, I was only trying to dry it. When the damp saturated my sleeping bag, I ended up spending the night huddled around a fire, half naked in minus temperatures trying to dry off my clothes to avoid hypothermia. To see it again, but under such different circumstances, was such a spin-out! I can't tell you how many times on my walk I'd said to myself, *The next time you see this place you'll be finished.* I was very sentimental, and it was touching to be back in spots where I could relive such vivid memories – almost surreal! I still hadn't processed it all being over yet.

I then drove to the north of Scotland to Dunnet Head, the most northerly point of the mainland, where I'd camped on the beach with the most incredible sunset. Each day, I spontaneously found myself making my way along the coast, often stopping off in places where I'd camped or even just where I recalled taking five minutes to take in the view. I can still remember everything, down to how I felt when I sat in each spot; no matter how knackered I was, it all just came flooding back like it was yesterday and I still felt like I was on the walk doing the same thing as ever. I made my way to Kinlochbervie on the northwest tip near Cape Wrath and camped up on a beach that I had once filmed on for the BBC, armed with firewood and a tent, and I spent my first night in what felt like so long feeling completely free! I skimmed stones into the sea and sat next to the fire just staring into it as I used to so often. But this time it was different; I was no longer looking down the stretch of coast and then checking my maps, working out the kind of day that was ahead of me – something that I'd done for so long! It felt less wholesome than it had when I was on the walk. Maybe it was because, this time, I was having a fire for the sake of it rather than out of necessity. This was the first sign, and maybe I had to just accept it, that life would never be the same again.

Over the next week as I revisited a whole load of places along the west coast of Scotland, including Skye, Mallaig, Glenfinnan, Fort William, Arisaig and lots more, I realized I hadn't written a word! Maybe I had used the second book's exile as an excuse to escape from it all – and everyone, including my little family. Though Kate had been on much of the walk, she had missed the earlier sections in the adventure that had been so magical to me – bloody hard, but magical. I'd had no one else to talk and relate to about any of it, apart from Jet, but she didn't say much!

Looking back as I sit here writing this in Scotland, I didn't come up here to write a book. That was never my intention, and I'm not ashamed to admit that I just needed a little bit of time to myself to process that my six-year endeavour was now over. I'm a much better thinker than I am a talker, so to sit in spots again where I'd once sat having absolutely no idea at the time of what this journey would end up giving me, allowed me to really reflect on it all. Day after day, week after week, month after month, and year after year, slowly but surely, after just putting one foot in front of the other, I had reached my goal. The goal wasn't the finish line; it was to find peace in myself and a purpose in my life once again.

We were still unsure exactly what it was that we wanted to do next, and the intensity of the walk towards the end hadn't really allowed us any time to even discuss it, but one thing that I did know was that the position that we were in, owning so little, was our greatest asset. We were not tied to anything. It's like the saying, 'If you have nothing, then you've got nothing to lose!' There was another blank sheet of paper in front of us soon enough to be filled with more adventures and ideas of a happy life for us. We had already proven to ourselves that we could achieve great things and were so excited to bring Magnus up to share in our future experiences and instil in him the belief that he had the potential to do anything.

Way back on the English coastline, we'd been fortunate enough to have been helped by some friends, Tobias and Rachel, whom we'd met on the journey and even spent a day fossil-hunting with down south – they'd even brought a bottle of bubbly to celebrate my book being a *Sunday Times* bestseller.

I drove the van to the end of a loch surrounded by mountains and, amazingly, was able to see the very spot where I'd camped a few days before my thirty-eighth birthday! I took out the tent once more and got foraging for firewood. It felt so good; I was so at home, more so than I had been in years! That craving for freedom had now been satisfied – all I needed now was the arrival of Kate and Magnus.

It was here that I finally accepted that it was all over, and that my work was done. I made a coffee over the fire and just sat and stared into the abyss. All I could hear were the screams of an eagle soaring above my head and the gentle lapping of the sea as it hit the shoreline. God, it was so peaceful. There was nobody around. It was just me and nature once again. Deep down, somehow, I knew I'd finish the book, and as I sit here writing this paragraph, I have done it! For the first time and for as long as I can remember, my sights have been taken off the walk and more on what we want to do next. So many ideas and so many dreams that I know we can make a reality. This adventure has taught me so much: the importance of self-belief, of throwing all of your eggs into one basket and just going for it; the kind of strength it takes to have the guts to break away from a lifestyle that is simply not for you; and having the tenacity and will to keep going until you reach what you want! It's funny, no matter how hard I try, the feeling of success at having completed my journey is nothing compared to the struggle it took to get there! That was the adventure: the journey!

Through good and through bad times, the focus always remained: never give up! You just can't if you want to be happy. I think of all these people I've met along the way who so often told me they wished they were doing some-thing like this and the only excuse I would ever accept is children (though this wasn't stopping us), disability or caring for a loved one in need. Truth be told, very few are prepared to give up the little comforts in life that we all take for granted. Not many are willing to risk losing everything. That's why there are so few out there like me, who truly understand that success does not come with the size of a house or how much you earn, but whether or not you wake up in the morning excited to get out there and do what you love doing. That's where true happiness lies. If you're true to yourself and pursue what makes you happy, then you're so much more likely to be lucky enough to find a like-minded partner who can share in it all with you. I really believe that if you put your heart and soul into something, regardless of how tiring and relentless it can be at times, or even if you just feel like it's impossible and you're completely rundown from trying, if the mindset is firing off the right cylinders, then nothing is impossible.

Throughout my life, I have always been interested in other people's beliefs, and I've come to realize that whether you believe in a God or whether you have belief in others around you, there is not a single belief out there that is more important than the belief in yourself. I completely understand that people need to look to others for faith and guidance at times, and that can be a good thing, but there is no validation more powerful and life-changing than the kind you get from yourself. I will never be that person to give up on something and brush it off with a simple, 'Oh well, it wasn't meant to be!' Sod that! It's like blaming someone else for you quitting. You must want something so much that failure is just not an option. All the crap stuff that happens along the way can only help you grow if you're thinking right, if you're prepared to learn from it, instead of dwelling on your misfortune! Bad things happen and people make mistakes. It's normal; it's life! And one only grows stronger when they realize that failing is not a crime; it's a lesson – and one of the best ones we can learn. I'd always remind myself of this as I watched Magnus go from crawling to walking. Each and every time he stood up and fell over, I would watch his face and I could see that determination. He just kept picking himself up and trying again, time after time until that day when he took his first steps and never looked back!

Modern life has become so hectic, so busy and so complicated and I believe that somewhere along the line we can lose that determination that is hardwired in us from such an early age. Imagine if we all approached our dreams and goals in the same way a baby approaches learning to walk. Each and every one of us would eventually succeed, I have absolutely no doubt.

The next morning, having packed away my camping gear and after probably the best night of sleep I'd had in years, I loaded up the van and sat on the shoreline having my cup of coffee as I stared at the surrounding mountains by one of Scotland's many beautiful lochs, ready to go to Comrie and rejoin my family.

I nodded my head at the landscape as a gesture of respect and gratitude for the incredible experiences I had had on this journey. I looked up at the sky, imagining Caitlin were here and wishing I could give her a hug.

Although she had not been with me physically, she had been in my head every single day and was my main driving force to complete this journey. She had challenged me to seek self-contentment and I realized that I had found happiness while on Hildasay. Now I had finally found the place I belonged – and it wasn't a house or a country or even a favourite spot. It was Jet, Kate and Magnus; they were my home. Nowhere would have been as special without them by my side.

A sense of comfort and stability surrounds me like a protective orb when we are all together, a feeling I've never had before and will protect with all that I have. And in the future, whenever I look at Kate, Magnus or Jet, I will always be reminded of an adventure so powerful and sentimental that words will never come close to describing it. A wholesome satisfaction that can only be earned from years of blood, sweat and tears, not handed down or given to me; a real achievement.

From this moment on, I vowed to always live for the now and be in the moment, to treat every day like it was my last. Too many times as I grow older, I see people plan so far ahead and sadly never make it that far, a tragedy that I can only learn from and try to never make the same mistake. It really is a rare and wonderful gift, this thing we call life.

I thought to myself as I turned away from the loch and made my way towards the van, that for the first time I was completely ready for whatever the future had in store for me; I was in control. Wherever I was to go from here and however life panned out, it was all down to me; the decisions I made, how I reacted to less fortunate situations, or how big I dared to dream. From now on I'd wait for nothing to come to me, or rely on anyone, or even entertain that word 'hope'. I was ready to take on a new challenge and it was up to me to make that happen.

With a big grin on my face, I started the engine to my old reliable T4 and glanced back at Jet to make sure she was comfortable. I set off in what was to my mind the last journey of Chris Walks the UK, to reunite with my family in Comrie and start our future together. God, I couldn't wait to see my little boy with that wonderful smile, and to give Kate a hug and tell her I loved her.

The butterflies and excitement in my stomach before I arrived were immense; of all the things up until now that I had done in my life, this was by far the greatest feeling of all. It was like a powerful magnet was drawing me to them; they were my safe place, my happy place, and together we could conjure up a future, dream big and make those wishes a reality. As I drove down the gravel track and saw the beaming smile on Magnus's face when I appeared from the van and he waded through the puddles to give his father a hug, an incredible feeling of pure joy shot through me. For the first time, my future was so bright; the fire inside continued to roar, and yet my body and mind were completely relaxed. A long cuddle from my wee man, along with the most warming smile coming from the beautiful eyes of Kate, who I am so proud to call my lady, was better than anything in the world.

We had booked a table at the Royal Hotel pub in Comrie, and I asked Kate to take Magnus and Jet down the short track that led to it, so I could go and grab a few bits we needed from the van. But that wasn't the real reason at all; I just wanted to see them all together. Kate took Jet's lead and Magnus's hand then started walking slowly away from me. I stood and got lost in their silhouettes. It was like my ears had blocked out any noise and my eyes saw nothing but the figures of a dog, a baby and a woman, walking happily together. As I took a deep breath ready to join them, it suddenly occurred to me that for the first time as an adult, I really loved life. The epic walk had given me a family, and my family were and always will be my home. At long last, I had found them.

I'll say this for the very last time. Have an absolute belter, folks!

Acknowledgements

I'm proud to be able to showcase some of the best of humanity in this book and I would like to thank all of you who supported us in any way along our journey. Kindness is what makes the world go around.

A special thank you to Elizabeth Barron for all your support over the past few years in times when we needed it. We would have been lost without you. Thank you so much – you're the best mother-in-law a man could ask for. Steve Roorke – you, mate, are the perfect example of helping because it feels good and want nothing in return. We could not have done this without you; you're a friend and a wonderful man. Our dear friend Anna Stiles – what a lovely woman you are. Your help all along the south coast was incredible! We always knew a quick phone call and you would be there. Above all you looked after my Jet through the night while Kate was in labour. We love you, pal, thank you. Ben Fogle – you went above and beyond to help us; you wrote the foreword for my first book and got us on your show, *New Lives in the Wild*, shooting our donations through the roof. Thank you for being on our side, mate. I can't thank you enough.

Mick – London was not an easy area to get around given our situation and it was you who made this all possible. You're salt of the earth and in my eyes one of the very best; thank you, my friend. Scott Miller – you saved my Jet's life. For that, I can't thank you enough. I hope we remain friends for ever. You're a good man and will always have such a special place in my heart. Thank you to Anne Robertson and Sarah Fowleigh; to Dean at Dub Daddy campers; to the lovely Shoenag from Inverness; and to Shona, my Instagram guru, thank you so much, pal. To the wonderful Nan and Rob. And my dear Caitlin, you were with me from start to finish. I love you so much.

Thank you to SSAFA for being so supportive along the journey. It was an honour to raise money for you. Thank you for being there for me. My editor and friend Richard Waters – you have a way of making me so at ease when I need it and have always believed in me and my writing. Any books I do in the future, I'd be honoured to work with you. Thank you, my friend.

Lastly, thank you to Kate, Jet and Magnus. Boy, this was not easy; many would have given up a long time ago, but knowing I needed to finish the walk, you all stood by my side through thick and thin no matter how tough it was. I love you all so much.

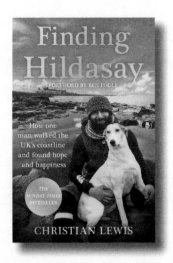

Finding Hildasay is Christian Lewis's brutal but beautiful true story of walking the coast of Britain – his dog Jet in tow – and finding a different way to live. With a foreword from longtime supporter Ben Fogle.

Ex-paratrooper Christian Lewis had hit rock bottom, suffering with depression so severe he would shut himself in his bedroom for weeks. Then while surfing – his sole respite – he cast his eyes along the coastline and realized it was the only place he really wanted to be.

Chris made an impulsive decision. He set himself a challenge: to walk the entire coastline of the UK. He gave himself a few days to rustle up a tent and walking boots, then left for good with just a tenner in his pocket and two days' worth of food. Little did he know at the time just how long it would take to cross the finish line – and the encounters lying ahead would turn his life around.